Staying Sane

Managing the

BOOKS

D1421569

© 2001 Tanya Arroba and Lesley Bell
Published by Age Concern England
1268 London Road
London SW16 4ER

First published 2001

Editor   Ro Lyon
Production   Vinnette Marshall
Design and typesetting   GreenGate Publishing Services
Printed in Great Britain by Bell & Bain Ltd, Glasgow

A catalogue record for this book is available from the British Library

ISBN 0–86242–267–1

Bulk orders
Age Concern England is pleased to offer customised editions of all its titles to UK
companies, institutions or other organisations wishing to make a bulk purchase.
For further information, please contact the Publishing Department at the address
on this page. Tel: 020 8765 7200. Fax: 020 8765 7211. Email: books@ace.org.uk

Contents

About the authors

Tanya Arroba is a chartered occupational psychologist who has spent a large part of her career being fascinated by the topic of stress at work. She started her career as a researcher for the Medical Research Council in the early days of stress research and discovered that people were more than happy to talk about the stress they faced at work. Tanya moved on to work in management development, and concentrated on the public sector, particularly local government, which brought her into contact with the world of social services and the caring professions. She developed an interest in how stress was manifest in the caring professions. Tanya runs her own management development consultancy, TAA, and also maintains her links with the University of Birmingham, where she has been associated with the Institute of Local Government Studies for over 20 years.

Lesley Bell has worked with social services and social care for over 25 years, specialising in the training of staff and managers and in the development of the organisations as a whole. Over this period she has seen major changes in the nature of the care services, in the way in which they are provided and in the roles and responsibilities assumed by individual managers and care staff. She has increasingly become aware of the strain this places upon people who are already undertaking stressful work in providing care for frail, vulnerable or dependent people. Lesley is Director of the not-for-profit company Initiatives in Care and is author of two best-selling books on domiciliary care for Age Concern England, *CareFully* (2nd edition) and *Managing CareFully*.

Tanya and Lesley have shared an interest in the world of social services since they met 20 years ago. This book is the end result of that shared interest.

Acknowledgements

There have been many people who have shared their experience with us over the years and many who have shared their thinking with us about stress and caring.

Our thanks go to everyone who has contributed to the development of our thinking although there are too many to thank personally.

Particular thanks go to Helen Petit for providing a base to complete the first draft. She provided a supportive and comfortable environment which was very conducive to thought and writing.

Tanya Arroba and **Lesley Bell**

Introduction

You have picked up this book, which indicates that you recognise the importance of managing stress in your own life, or the working lives of those around you. In this introduction we look at who we are writing this book for and at why it is important to be aware of stress. Finally we outline what this book can do for you and how it can help you to address some of the problems you may be facing.

Who this book is for

This book is written for people who spend their time caring for adults and older people. It is aimed particularly at those people whose paid work involves providing care – either directly or as managers or trainers – or those responsible for developing services. It may also be of use to people who care for others as part of unpaid family or friendship responsibilities. We are aware that demands and pressures vary in each of the different settings in which care is provided. We also believe that the pressures of work experienced in any care environment are sufficiently similar to warrant addressing the topic of the stress of caring as an issue in its own right.

An increasing number of people survive into old age, with a correspondingly greater need for care services. As a result the need and demand for people to provide care for others will continue to increase, as will the demands of being a carer. It is the demands of being a carer and the need to manage these demands which form the focus of this book.

Why it is important to be aware of stress

It is only relatively recently that stress has started being taken seriously in the world of work. Previously the notion of stress was viewed with some suspicion and regarded as something that only 'wimps' suffered. Now stress is becoming a respectable research topic, and is seen as an area which needs to be taken seriously.

Employers are increasingly sensitive to the demands stress makes on individuals, and on the efficiency of their business. Stress-related problems indicate that all is not well for the individual, but equally, that all is not well where they work. Far too many working days are lost because of stress-related illness. As far back as 1986, Kearns suggested that '100 million days are lost every year because people cannot face going to work' (Newell 1995).

As knowledge of what happens when stress is around has grown, it has become evident that it can be manifest in many different ways. The phrase 'stress-related illness' is one which is heard more and more and has entered the everyday vocabulary. Doctors are more aware of the effects of stress and many sick notes refer to stress as a reason for absence from work. Stress not only causes physical illness but is also linked to mental and psychological discomfort. In recent years there have been some landmark court cases, beginning with a High Court judgement against Northumberland County Council in 1994, where a social worker took his employer to court for damages for stress. This would have been unheard of only a few years previously. Apart from establishing the principle that employers have a duty of care to provide a safe working environment emotionally and psychologically, it firmly places stress under the Health and Safety legislation. The promotion of physical well-being at work has long been viewed as the responsibility of all employers, and the right of every employee. Now well-being has been expanded to include psychological and emotional well-being too. This means that every employer has to take account of the stress aspect of all work.

As awareness has grown of the demands of being a carer, so awareness has increased that the providing of personal and physical care is work which can all too easily become stressful. If stress is present, it is all too easy to lose sight of the rewards of being a carer and only be aware of the demands: work which is potentially so rewarding can be overshadowed by feelings of stress.

So, stress needs to be taken seriously because:

- the demand for care has increased;
- there are more carers;

- the right of employees to a safe working environment has been recognised;
- there is increased knowledge about how stress affects work; and
- there is better recognition that caring work is demanding.

Yet there are two even more important reasons for taking the time to consider how to manage your stress as a carer. These are firstly, the fact that if you are stressed you will not be in a position to provide the most effective care you are capable of giving. The quality of the caring you provide will inevitably diminish if you are stressed, and indeed you may well pass on your stress to the person for whom you are caring. Secondly, if you are experiencing stress, it will at the very least be an uncomfortable experience and at worst a damaging one for you. Therefore, in the interests of the well-being of the people you care for, as well as your own health, it is vitally important to be aware of stress and its effects as an issue for you.

What this book can do for you

We feel strongly that stress can be a very real issue for those who provide care for others. However, we are also aware that there are a lot of myths surrounding this topic. Therefore our first aim in this book is to demystify the topic of stress. Our objective is that you should become clearer and feel better informed in general about stress.

We are also aware that for many years there was a stigma attached to the discussion of stress – and nowhere was this more in evidence than in the world of the caring professions. Whilst most people would accept that stress in itself is undesirable, any consideration that carers themselves might become stressed was taboo. Paradoxically it was quite legitimate to talk about the stress experienced by those being cared for. We hope that as a result of reading this book you, as a carer, will feel more comfortable acknowledging the possibility of stress in your caring role and able to consider it and discuss it without feeling worried.

Above all, this book is about how to manage the stress which may be present for you in your caring role. Information and an open mind are necessary, but the most important element is to feel that there are techniques and skills which you can use to manage your stress. Increased awareness on its own can just add to the pressures. Therefore, we want you to feel more aware of how to manage your stress as a result of reading this book. We also hope that you might be more aware of how to respond to stress in others you manage or work alongside.

How to use this book

Our starting point is to demystify what happens when stress is around. In Chapter 1 we look at the mechanics of stress and how it occurs and provide a basic understanding of the topic and dispel some of the myths.

In Chapter 2 we look at how the word stress has become a value-laden term and how this can get in the way of managing it productively. Stress affects us all in different ways; something you had managed competently may unexpectedly become a source of stress to you, such as change in your working patterns, or greater workloads, or the care of a person close to death. We encourage recognition of any unhelpful attitudes and support the concept of stress as simply a fact of life. This approach will provide a firm foundation for considering how to manage it.

In Chapter 3 we look at the first skill of managing stress, which is the skill of recognising when there is stress around for you. We look at the sources of information available and take you through some steps to help you become more familiar with recognising your own stress.

In Chapter 4 we look at the demands which the role of being a carer can place on you. Identifying the demands is a useful starting point. We introduce the notion that sometimes we can create additional pressure for ourselves by our own views and thoughts. In particular we look at the pressures which carers can place on themselves.

In Chapter 5 we begin the process of identifying whether the demands and pressures you face as a carer are necessary or unnecessary. We introduce the notion of reducing unnecessary pressure as a key skill in managing stress.

In Chapter 6 we turn our attention to considering what you need to do to increase your resilience and keep yourself afloat amidst the demands you face as a carer. We consider where you get rewards and positive experiences in your life as a whole and encourage you to consider ways to increase them. We focus on two specific areas that will help you manage your 'pressure balance' – these are support and training. We examine each one and look at ways in which you can ensure that you get the support you need and identify the training which will help you feel more confident. Managers can develop and pass on the same techniques to help their staff.

In Chapter 7 we offer some useful techniques for reducing stress once it occurs. You should always keep a watchful eye on your pressure balance. Finding the pressure levels that are right for you is not something you can sort out once and for all; stress management is a continual process. Hopefully it is something that becomes second nature as you become more practised and we will encourage you to plan for that in Chapter 8. Throughout the book we have included activities to help you put into practice the skills and techniques we describe.

We have introduced you to the topic and to the book. We hope that we have given the message that stress is not something that is inevitable and has to be endured. It can be managed so that you as a carer, and the people you provide care for, can all benefit. We also hope that as a paid carer your employer will give you every support in this.

KEY POINTS

- Stress is an important topic for everyone to understand.
- This book is for you if you provide care for adults or older people, particularly if that is your paid work.
- This book is also for you if you manage or provide training for carers.
- The demand for carers is increasing.
- The demands of care work are increasing.
- More is known now about the harmful effects of stress at work.
- If you are experiencing stress you will be less effective in your work as a carer.
- This book can help to demystify stress and provide a basic understanding.
- This book can provide techniques and skills to manage stress.

1 Understanding how stress works

Caring can be a stimulating and rewarding experience, but to reap its rewards over time (and to help others do so too), it helps to know how stress affects you. In this chapter we will look at exactly what stress is and how historical factors influence the stress we experience today.

What is stress?

In all areas of our lives we are faced with demands. From the moment we wake up we have to respond to whatever the day brings. Imagine a day which starts by oversleeping, because, for some reason, the alarm clock has failed to go off. Then there is a traffic jam and the car, which has been unreliable for some time, decides to pack up completely, leaving you stranded with some way to go before your first call. There may be all sorts of things going around in your mind at that moment, all sorts of feelings churning around inside you – but is it stress?

As human beings we have the ability to respond to the demands that are made on us. We have a brain, which processes information which comes in through the senses and enables us to make decisions, and we have emotions which enable us to respond to the world of other people. In fact as human beings we need a certain level of stimulation in order to work well and feel good. Imagine a situation where there were no demands, no pressures to be dealt with. Initially it would seem lovely, simply to have the time to relax and catch your breath. However if this situation continued day after day, month after month, it would soon cease to be such an idyllic situation and the chances are that boredom would creep in. The first few days of a holiday can be a difficult time, as we learn to adjust to a different pace. It is often at the start of a holiday that people go down with minor infections, such as colds. It seems that once the pressure is off, the body allows itself to unwind and feel some of what has been happening.

In a series of experiments many years ago, a group of people were deprived of any stimulation through the senses. They were immersed in tanks of lukewarm water, fed white noise (that is noise played at an even volume and pitch to provide no variation in sensory input) through headphones, and blindfolded with goggles. This was known as a situation of sensory deprivation. Each person was equipped with a panic button and the idea was to see what happened when no input through the senses was allowed. Many different things were experienced but the one factor which was common was that no-one could stand it for very long – they became stressed. We need stimulation and we are designed to deal with it.

Therefore, if as humans we need stimulation, when does stimulation become stressful? To put it very simply, we have a basic need for a certain level of stimulation and pressure. It becomes stressful when the level of pressure and demand is either too much or, perhaps surprisingly, when it is too little.

The sum of all the demands we face at any given time adds up to our pressure level. When the pressure level is too low, our attention is distracted and we mentally go off the boil. It is very difficult to maintain a sharp focus and feel energetic if there is not much happening around us to stimulate us. The stress of **boredom** sets in.

At the other extreme, when we are bombarded with demands – demanding clients, tight deadlines, bad traffic, demands from the family – we feel overwhelmed and overloaded. This is when the pressure level is too high for us. When there is too much pressure, too many demands, we experience the stress of **overload**.

There have been many definitions given over the years for stress. In this book we will use a simple definition which is '**that stress is the response to an inappropriate level of pressure**'.

The word **inappropriate** is the key to understanding stress. Every person needs an appropriate level of pressure, for that is when we function at our best. There is a gap between boredom and overload where we experience a level of pressure and demand which is just right for us. That level will be different for each one of us. When we reach that 'optimum' level, there is no stress, just a healthy and appropriate level of stimulation. This is the target for stress management. The aim is to spend as much time in this **zone of optimum pressure** as possible. The key is that the pressure level is appropriate for the person. The diagram below illustrates what happens at different pressure levels:

HIGH PRESSURE = Overload
ZONE OF OPTIMUM PRESSURE
LOW PRESSURE = Boredom

There is, however, no easy or simple way of telling exactly when pressure turns into stress. Put two people in what appears to be the same situation and one may well experience stress whereas the other will not. Stress is very much an individual matter. It is really only by the response to the situation that stress can be measured. Much work has been done on measuring stress, ranging from taking physiological measures of muscle tension and biochemicals in the bloodstream, to self-reports using questionnaires. In Chapter 3 we will look at how to recognise stress in yourself. At this stage we simply want to point out that it can be difficult to tell when stress happens, although we get a clearer idea of what might be happening if we break our basic definition of stress into three component parts.

The three components of stress

There are three components, which add up to determine if stress will be experienced. The diagram below shows how they interact. We will be working with these three factors throughout this book. Here we will say a little more about what we mean.

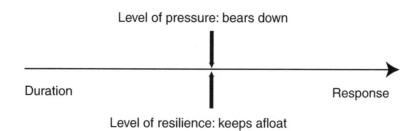

Level of pressure: bears down

Duration

Response

Level of resilience: keeps afloat

The level of pressure

The first component is the level of pressure that is experienced. This is the sum of all the demands that you face, whether they are demands in your work as a carer or in other areas of your life. Very few people keep their life in neat and separate compartments. Pressure experienced in any area of life will have a knock-on effect on other areas. Moreover, many pressures we experience come from our own thinking: we are very capable of putting pressure on ourselves; we do not always need other people or the outside world to do it for us. However, the level of pressure experienced is only one part of the picture. There are two other factors which make up the jigsaw which leads to stress.

The level of resilience

As human beings we are resilient in the face of the demands placed on us. It is our resilience that keeps us afloat. There are various factors that affect the level of resilience we experience at any given time. These factors can take many different forms, including facets of our personality, past experience, confidence levels, skill levels and the quality of support in our lives. They combine to determine whether we encounter daily pressures feeling resourceful and resilient, or struggle to stay afloat from the start. If we have a good foundation of 'resilience-enhancing' factors, we will be able to deal with a greater level of demand before it becomes stressful. On the other hand, if we are not quite so resilient, it will not take as much pressure to push us under and for stress to set in. However, there is one further factor that completes the picture.

How long the pressure lasts

Most people have had the experience of the odd rushed day, perhaps when a colleague is off sick, a client is particularly demanding or the car breaks down. Occasional crises, occasional times when the pressure level mounts, are not in themselves very problematic. If our resilience level is good we can usually rise to the occasion and deal with the odd time of high pressure. It is not the increase in pressure itself that will cause stress, but how long it lasts. It is when the level of pressure is too high, or too low, for a period of time that the problems really begin. When left unmanaged for a prolonged period of time, an inappropriate level of pressure is in fact dangerous. We will expand on what we mean by dangerous as we outline what can happen when stress is around.

How the stress response came about

The origin of the stress response is lost in the mists of time but is generally believed to have been part of our prehistoric ancestors' repertoire for dealing with difficulties. It has been referred to as a 'basic survival pack' for the human race. Whenever our ancestors encountered a large, dangerous beast, they needed to act quickly to survive. As soon as the threat had been perceived, the internal alarm button was activated and the person geared up to either run to get away from the danger, or to fight and destroy the opposition. It has become known as the 'fight or flight' response. Fighting or running are both very good survival tactics when faced with a woolly mammoth or sabre-toothed tiger. The availability of this response ensured the survival of the human race. Although it still stands us in good stead, the ways which were helpful to our ancestors are less likely to be of such good use to us today.

Yet we do still encounter situations where there is not time to consider all available options. Crossing a road when a car suddenly comes straight towards you is not a moment for testing your powers of logical and rational decision making, or calling a working party to assess the options. It is time to move quickly, preferably to take avoiding action by running. We do still need to have the ancient response available, but problems arise when it is triggered inappropriately.

Facing your boss who is angry about something you have done may well feel very similar to facing a charging mammoth. Dealing with a client who seems intent on undermining you, and does nothing but criticise, may well bring out the urge to fight or turn tail and flee. In your work as a carer, you will not encounter real beasts, but you will encounter many situations which feel just the same.

In order to prepare to run or fight, a whole host of physical changes take place. The diagram below shows this in summary.

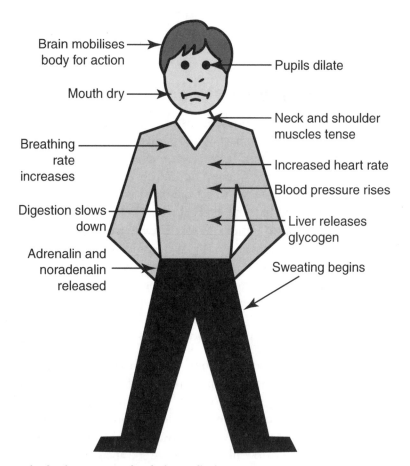

How the body prepares for fight or flight

In effect, all attention goes on what is needed to run quickly or fight effectively. So the blood pumps faster to get the fuel needed to the large muscle groups of the arms and legs. The heart rate increases and breathing becomes more shallow and rapid to ensure a good intake of oxygen. The muscles in the shoulder and neck tighten and the body weight is swung forward onto the balls of the feet to enable either running or fighting. The digestive system slows down, as food is not the priority when facing danger. There may be a 'butterfly' sensation in the stomach and sweating begins.

When looking at all the changes which take place to enable us to survive a threat by running or fighting, it is possible to see why some of the changes occur when we face stress today – the increase in muscle tension, the racing heart, the feelings of anxiety, of anger, or of wanting to withdraw. We may not physically throw a punch, but we can be short-tempered and irritable. We have learnt to fight with words or gestures rather than fists. Equally we may not literally turn on our heels and rush out of the door, but we may become more withdrawn and feel less like communicating. We can withdraw into ourselves even if we do not take flight.

The problems come when we trigger the fight or flight response inappropriately; either it is not the equivalent of a dangerous beast, or we trigger it too often. We are designed to encounter the odd nasty beast, which is why we were equipped with a survival mechanism. We are *not* designed to have the resilience to constantly face mammoths all day, every day. We will look at this in Chapter 5 in more detail when we identify how unnecessary pressure can be reduced. The point we want to emphasise here is what happens when we trigger the fight/flight response too often: the changes which occur and which are designed to get us out of a tight spot are not designed to become a way of life. It is when we trigger this response too often that the changes can endanger our health and lead to stress-related illness.

Earlier we made the point that if left unmanaged for too long, stress can be dangerous. The danger happens when, for example:

- There is too much adrenalin or cholesterol coursing round the system, providing a fertile ground for heart problems.

- The digestive system has to deal with food whilst other parts of the system are facing mammoths, providing a fertile ground for digestive tract problems.
- The immune system slows down and can no longer work as well, making us more prone to colds or even, at the worst, to cancers.

The exact pathways between stress and subsequent illnesses are still being explored, but it is now known beyond doubt that prolonged experience of stress is linked to physical illness (Rice 1999).

KEY POINTS

- Stress is the response to an inappropriate level of pressure.
- Pressure is the sum of all the demands faced at any given time.
- The level of demand faced is the first component of stress.
- Our level of resilience is the second component.
- How long the pressure lasts is the third component.
- Underpinning the personal pattern are the physical changes linked to our prehistoric 'stress response', which gears us up to 'fight or flight'.
- When left unmanaged the physical changes associated with stress can lead to illness.

---

2 Attitudes to stress

In this chapter we will look at the variety of attitudes held about stress which either help, or get in the way of, recognising when it is present. We move on in the next chapter to look at the skill of recognising stress.

Stress is emotive

Stress is a term originally used in the engineering profession to denote the effects of pressure on materials. In engineering, stress was simply a case of looking to see what happened to various substances when pressure was exerted on them. There was no expectation that one substance rather than another would be able to take a higher stress load, nor were there judgements made when it was found that the stress-bearing capacity was different in different materials. The information was simply used in planning which material to use for different purposes. The exercise for engineers was a purely objective and scientific one, gaining information and using it in the course of their professional work.

However, from the early days of interest in the topic of stress at work it became evident that stress is not a neutral word when used in connection with people. It quickly became a judgemental comment to point to a particular person or group of people and say that they could not carry a great deal of pressure; they were 'stressed out'.

ACTIVITY 1

Reading is never a passive activity, as you are thinking all the time. However putting those thoughts into your own words, and not necessarily into words that you've read, helps you clarify your own thoughts about the subject. We suggest that you take a few moments to complete the following exercise to draw out the attitudes you hold about stress.

List all the thoughts that come to mind about what stress is, or is not, for you. You may find many thoughts come to mind, or only one. What is important is not the number but the identification of your own thoughts and attitudes to stress.

Complete the following sentences

In my view stress is --

In my view stress is --

In my view stress is --

In my view stress is not --

In my view stress is not --

In my view stress is not --

Look at what you have written and notice what you are saying about how you view stress. Are you tending to view it in a negative light as something to be ashamed of; or are you seeing it as a status symbol; or are you viewing it as a fact of modern life?

You can see from this simple exercise that considering stress in people, particularly in the workplace, is a highly emotive subject. The attitudes held about stress range from viewing it as a negative comment on someone's ability, to the other extreme of it becoming a status symbol. These attitudes will influence how easy or otherwise it is to acknowledge and talk about personal stress, particularly when you are a carer.

Stress as a sign of weakness

Twenty years ago, as stress was just beginning to be taken seriously in the workplace, it was not uncommon for researchers to be met with such statements as 'there is no stress here, we are all competent people' or 'when the going gets tough, the tough get going'. This was initially a rather baffling response, until the link between stress and weakness was taken into account. It appeared that there was a strong prevailing view that stress was a sign of weakness, and that someone who suffered or admitted to stress, was somehow inadequate or incompetent.

The words 'suffer stress' in themselves suggest that this is something with which a person is afflicted. It is something that is therefore seen as an unusual occurrence. A tendency to suffer stress is a weakness, a little like an allergy or some other disabling factor. If a person suffers stress, that must make them less able to work well.

The reverse side of this view therefore, is that people do not normally suffer stress. The person who does suffer it is the odd one out, as most people manage perfectly well and are not prone to suffer stress. Thus suffering stress is a sign of weakness and something to be ashamed of. This attitude was clear in the reluctance to attend workshops on stress management which was a feature in the early days: attending a stress management programme was tantamount to admitting that you were one of that odd bunch of people who suffered stress.

'Admit to stress' again conjures up how difficult it can be to acknowledge that you experience stress. 'Admit' gives the ring of admitting to some crime, owning up to something which is not quite nice. After all, if stress is only something that happens to weak or inadequate people, then it is not a good idea to admit to it, because that is the same as making a public statement of inadequacy.

The reluctance to admit to stress was clear in the numbers of people who said that they would not feel easy talking to their line manager about stress. This was stated very clearly indeed when a police authority was setting up an early counselling scheme. The idea was that all employees of that authority would have someone to talk to when the pressure got too much. In the awareness training which preceded the setting up of the counselling service, the overwhelming view was that it would never do to admit to stress publicly because that admission would get on to your personal record, and be held against you in promotion panels. That view might have been at its most extreme in the police service, but the reluctance to admit to stress because it carried stigma was widespread.

If the view is held that stress is something to be ashamed of, people will keep very quiet about it. If recognising the presence of stress carries with it a blow to self-esteem, then this will not make it easy to use the first skill of stress management – recognising when stress is present.

There can be a lot of denial and clinging to the notion that being effective means never 'suffering stress'.

Views have changed over the years and it is now more acceptable to talk about stress. Stress is not the closet subject it once was, and yet in some workplaces a link is still sometimes made between the presence of stress and personal inadequacy. Managers can play a crucial role in creating the kind of 'climate' where stress can be acknowledged without any implication of incompetence. Effective managers will openly acknowledge and manage their own pressure levels and encourage their staff in supervision and management sessions to talk about aspects of their work that they find stressful.

As far as we are concerned, **stress is something that can be experienced by anybody.** Nobody is immune to experiencing inappropriate pressure. Stress is a fact of life and not something to be ashamed of.

However, another commonly held view, which we will explore further now, is that stress is actually a status symbol.

Stress as a status symbol

When organisations were approached in the early days of stress research there was frequently an alternative view put forward – '*do come and study stress here. We are all stressed as we are all hard-working people*'. That view gave the message that somehow stress was seen as part and parcel of the life of busy, hard-working people, especially managers – a 'badge of honour'.

The idea of stress as akin to a status symbol is illustrated by the reluctance of a senior manager to admit that he did not feel stressed. He seemed to be puzzled by the fact that he was holding down a senior job in a busy local authority department, apparently doing it well, and was not experiencing stress symptoms. This may have been an extreme example, but it does illustrate that stress is often considered to be an inevitable consequence of holding senior, responsible positions.

Although there has been much interest in the stress levels of managers, it has long been known that stress is not the preserve of those with managerial responsibility alone. Depending upon the nature of the work, stress levels can be higher amongst front-line staff than among senior managers.

Unfortunately, some managers have held the mistaken belief that part of their role is to make sure that staff are stressed. They took the view that stress leads to better work; a myth we discussed in Chapter 1. Sometimes, however, they simply thought that stress and hard work were inextricably linked; therefore, when staff were working hard, they would automatically be stressed.

As few people like to be viewed as other than hard-working, it is not surprising that there is quite a strong view that stress is a good thing, a badge of hard work, something to be aimed for. We have heard people appear to almost boast about their stress symptoms, and even to appear to look down on people who were not showing signs of stress. A view of stress as something to boast about will, however, lead to an exaggeration of stress symptoms, and a biased view of what is really happening.

We believe that stress is certainly not something to boast about, any more than it is something to be ashamed of. Think back to the way that pressure, resilience and time act on each other (see page 4). **Stress is not an inevitable part of working life, nor is it something that just has to be put up with.**

We take the view that stress is a fact of life. It occurs when the pressure level is wrong and denying its existence on the one hand, or exaggerating it on the other, merely makes it more difficult to recognise. Recognition is the first skill and anything which gets in the way of that will make life more difficult when it comes to managing stress.

Attitudes to stress when you are a carer

Acknowledging stress when you spend your time caring for others raises a different set of views and attitudes which again can hinder recognition. The attitudes towards stress when you are a carer are complex. There are many different reasons why people take on caring roles, and each of those reasons has its own links to stress and its recognition.

Caring as a profession

The decision to enter the caring professions and spend your life and career as a carer is often based on a deep-seated wish to help others who are in need. By definition the perceived role of a carer involves doing things for others which they are not able to do for themselves. This casts the carer as the person who can do things, and the person to whom care is provided as the one who has needs. The carer is there to meet those needs. It is then relatively easy to slip into thinking that dedication to the role of carer means putting the other person's needs above all else, including your own needs. There is a basic human need for a certain level of stimulation and pressure and it can at times be tempting to overlook this when meeting the service user's needs. There is a possibility that needs are seen as acceptable on the part of the other person but not on your part. This will make it harder to acknowledge that your need, as a carer, is to work with appropriate levels of pressure and make it difficult when the pressure level is not right for you.

Sometimes being a carer is seen as being selfless, in which case discounting personal need is highly prized. This will not encourage the recognition of stress; that requires both an acceptance of the basic need for right amounts of pressure, and an acknowledgement that difficulties follow when pressures are wrong. Organisations need codes of practice which set staff 'boundaries' and make it clear that managers must act once inappropriate pressure levels trigger stress-related problems.

Caring as a job

If you regard caring simply as a way of earning a living – a job, rather than a career – then it is less likely that you will be tempted to discount your own needs. Your past experience in various other jobs may have influenced the way you view pressure. You may even have taken up caring because you saw it as less highly pressured than other jobs you have held. If you view caring as a job rather than a vocation, you may be less weighed down by expectations around stress.

Caring as a duty

If you have entered caring out of a sense of duty, then it is likely that this will discourage you from admitting to difficulty with the pressure encountered. The notion of duty often carries with it a feeling of lack of choice, a sense that you sometimes have to do things. This may apply particularly when the caring is provided in family situations. The feeling of duty itself may well be one of the pressures experienced. Feeling as if you have little or no option, and also perhaps feeling weighed down by duty, is a difficult situation to be in. Even if stress is acknowledged, there is little sense of a way out. If there is a feeling of being trapped, then it can be painful to acknowledge the stress, because what then do you do with it?

This scenario is illustrated vividly in the case of a middle-aged woman caring for her husband with Alzheimer's disease. As the man became increasingly disorientated, the children of the couple became more concerned about the pressure that was building up on their mother. One of the sons investigated the situation and found that there were ways in which his mother could get some help and some relief. This help could come in practical forms, as well as in the help offered by a local support group. The son went to see his mother to talk about managing her pressure, only to be met by a complete denial of any need for help. It was her duty to care for her husband, and that was that. No amount of persuasion could get her even to address the fact that she might be finding it difficult, let alone encourage her to look at practical solutions.

An article on the roles of the Occupational Therapist (in the December 1996/January 1997 newsletter of the Alzheimer's Society) identified one of those roles as giving advice on stress management for the carer. This is really important, but will not get very far if the carer, bound by duty, refuses to recognise any need for stress management. Neither Occupational Therapist nor family member can make someone take stress management on board. We cannot help someone deal with stress unless they recognise that stressful parts of their lives are something others could help them manage. The Alzheimer's Society and other carer's groups play a major role in providing support to carers and reducing the stress of caring.

Identifying your own attitudes to stress

We have looked at some of the attitudes which can either help or hinder a recognition of when stress is happening. These attitudes may:

- be embedded in the culture of the organisation for which you work;
- form part of the unwritten rules of how things are done and be a backdrop to your work as a carer; or
- they may be your own attitudes towards stress.

We would like to invite you to reflect on your attitudes, to identify what they are, and to see whether they help or hinder you from taking the first step towards managing stress; recognising that it is around for you. Think back to Activity 1 at the beginning of this chapter (pages 10–11). Is there anything you wrote there, that, having read this chapter, you would now want to write differently?

Now that we have looked at the effects of different attitudes towards stress and have encouraged you to take the view that stress is nothing to be ashamed of, nothing to boast about, and certainly not something to deny just because you are a carer, it is time to move on to the next step in managing stress. The next step is to look at how to recognise stress in yourself.

KEY POINTS

- Stress is an emotive topic.
- It is possible to hold attitudes towards stress which can get in the way of managing it.
- Stress is still often viewed as a sign of weakness.
- Stress is sometimes viewed as a status symbol.
- Unhelpful attitudes are around about admitting to stress as a carer.
- It is helpful to recognise that stress is a fact of life and nothing to be ashamed of.

---

3   Recognising when stress is present

In this chapter we move on to look at the first skill of managing stress, which is the ability to recognise when stress is around for you – starting with Activity 2 below.

ACTIVITY 2

This exercise is designed to start you thinking about those occasions when stress is present for you.

Make a list of some of the work and leisure activities that make physical, mental or psychological demands on you. Tick the 'not stressful' box if the activity is one that you seldom, or never, associate with stress for you; tick the 'stressful' box if you've listed an activity you often associate with stress; and tick the 'either' box if you think the experience is sometimes stressful, and sometimes not.

Activities	Not stressful	Stressful	Either

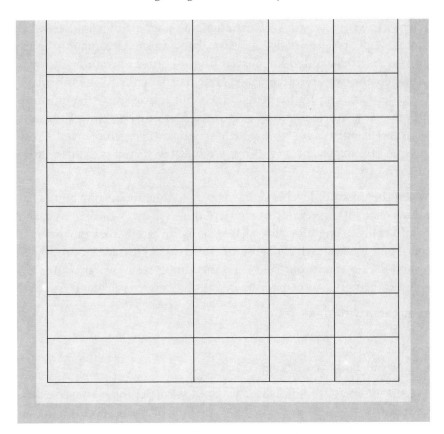

We now go on to explore what happens when stress occurs and will come back to exploring your own personal response.

What happens when stress occurs

There are many stereotypes of what happens when someone is stressed. There is the image of the person tearing their hair out as they rush from one thing to the next. There is the image of the person falling into the pub after a hard day, downing a few drinks and falling out of the pub before collapsing into bed. Whatever the stereotypes, the reality is that there are many ways in which stress is manifested. In the early days of stress research a great deal of researchers' time was spent trying to find the definitive checklist of stress symptoms. Helpful though it would be, there is no such thing.

There are as many ways of experiencing and manifesting stress as there are people, in theory at least. The response to inappropriate pressure is a very individual matter. In the course of training in stress management, we are often asked 'Is what happens to me, normal?' We take that as a plea for reassurance, but it does raise the question of what is a 'normal' stress response. A normal stress response is whatever is normal for you, which may bear no resemblance to how anyone else experiences it. Now we will try to unravel this a little further.

When the pressure level is right for us, we function at our best. That means that in all areas of our functioning we are working well and comfortably, using all our available skills. It means that our mind is sharp and focused, we feel good in ourselves, we behave appropriately and skilfully and our body is functioning well. We are, after all, complex beings. We are made up of various different elements, such as:

- our ability to think;
- how we feel;
- what we do; and
- how our body is working.

These four areas are simply one way of looking at the whole complex system which is the human being. When the pressure level is right, all areas are working well. When the pressure level moves away from the optimum for us, then changes start to occur.

These changes can be experienced or show themselves in any area of our functioning. For example, one person we knew learnt to recognise that whenever the pressure level was not right for her, it affected her mental functioning most. She found that her brain felt fuzzy and clogged up, that her memory was affected and that her ability to make decisions was impaired. Another person described stress purely in terms of the changes in feelings he became aware of. When stress was around for him, he began to feel anxious and less confident and got angry at the smallest things, which he saw as slights. A different person may experience no changes in the mental or emotional areas at all, but find themselves behaving differently.

Often it is comments from other people which can draw our attention to changes in our behaviour. For example, a common change in behaviour when stress is around is snapping at colleagues or service users, and generally being more short-tempered. Having difficulty sleeping is an often mentioned indicator of stress for many people. Other people recognise that stress is around by changes in their physical well-being and talk of headaches or aches and pains in the muscles.

The key word is **change**. In order to recognise when stress is around, you need to become aware of the changes which are occurring. The change can happen in one or more of our areas of functioning, as illustrated in the lists below:

Changes in mental functioning

- difficulty in absorbing information
- difficulty in maintaining concentration
- attention wandering
- difficulty making decisions
- judgement being impaired

Changes in behaviour

- poor time-keeping
- drinking more alcohol
- having difficulty sleeping
- more aggressive behaviour
- less communicative

Changes in emotions

- feeling anxious
- loss of self-confidence
- feeling panicky
- feeling irritable
- feeling short-tempered

Physical changes

- strained back
- headaches and migraines
- indigestion and digestive difficulties
- susceptibility to colds and bugs
- increased heart rate

ACTIVITY 3

Refer back to the activities you identified as stressful for you in Activity 2 (see page 18). Consider each one and see if you can recognise any of the changes listed above as occurring when you undertake those activities.

Each person will have their own individual and, at times, idiosyncratic ways of responding when the pressure level is not right for them. Underneath whatever the personal response is, and whatever changes that brings about, is the physiological reaction we described in Chapter 1, 'the stress response'. We can see the ways in which the prehistoric response to run or to fight can be translated into changes in behaviour today. The key point is to recognise that how you respond when the pressure is not right for you is a combination of the ancient stress response and your personal pattern of responding to pressure levels.

Recognising signs of stress

Knowing the origin of the stress response, and the way that inappropriate pressure leads to changes in any area of human functioning, leads on to the first skill of stress management – recognising when stress is happening to you.

Often, if the pressure has been mounting for some time, your system will take matters into its own hands, so to speak, and you will experience physical or emotional symptoms. The aim is to recognise at an early point when the pressure level is moving away from one that is right for you. Sometimes the shift can be quite gradual and not accompanied by major trauma. In this case it is more difficult to detect when stress is starting to creep in. It is important that we use the sources of information available to us to pinpoint the onset of stress. Caught at an early stage, we can manage stress better. We will be looking in later chapters at ways of doing this. If left to a later stage, there is usually little energy left for doing much that is constructive; it simply becomes a matter of survival.

There are three sources of information available to help you become more able to pinpoint when you are experiencing stress. These are:

- what other people tell you that they are observing in your behaviour;
- knowing your pattern from your past experience; and
- being able to monitor yourself for what is happening, as it happens.

Listening to what others tell you

People around you only have access to your behaviour. They cannot know what is happening in your thoughts or feelings, or how you are feeling physically – unless you tell them. Others may pick up changes in your behaviour when you are not aware of them yourself. You may need someone else to help you see how those changes affect the quality of your work. Often, when we are feeling particularly hard-pressed, we concentrate on getting on with the jobs on the list, and lose our awareness of what we are doing. It can feel a little like going on to automatic pilot. So it can come as quite a surprise when other people point out quite what our behaviour looks like from their point of view. The more someone has a chance to get to know your usual behaviour patterns, the more chance there is that they will detect a change. It can be very useful information, and we would encourage you to invite comments from others, without feeling defensive.

Recognising your pattern from the past

You will have encountered times in your past when the pressure level was not right for you, as well as times when it was just right. By reflecting on your past experience, you will be able to detect the changes which make up your personal response to stress. This will be useful information that helps you know what to watch out for in future.

ACTIVITY 4

The first step in this activity is to bring to mind three occasions you have already experienced:

- a time when the pressure level was low;

- a time when the pressure level was high; and

- a time when the pressure level was just right for you.

At this point we would encourage you to focus your attention on what it felt like to be you at each of those times. It is less important now to look at what the pressures were; we will come on to that later in the book. At the moment, all we invite you to bring to mind is what your experience was at each of those three times. When you've done that, we'll move on.

Can you now recall what your experience was in each of the following areas?

- How clearly were you thinking and how was your mind working?

- How did you feel?

- What about your behaviour? What were you doing?

- What was happening to you physically, and how did your body feel?

Jot down some notes on a spare piece of paper, and then see if you can detect any patterns. Then fill in the following sentences:

When the pressure level is low for me,

I --

When the pressure level is high for me,

I --

When the pressure level is right for me,

I --

Now refer back to Activities 2 and 3 (on pages 18 and 22) and put together the information you have gathered on what actually happens to you when you experience stress.

Monitoring changes as they happen

Equipped with feedback from those around you about any changes they have noticed in your behaviour, *and* being clear about the patterns you have picked up from reflecting on your past experience of different pressure levels, we move now to the final source of information.

You should now have a clear idea of the changes that you experience and manifest when the pressure level is wrong. All that remains is for you to become more aware of those changes as they happen, and to acknowledge that perhaps the pressure level is not quite right for you.

If you use the information you get about your personal stress response as a starting point for doing something to manage your pressure level, you will be better able to deal with stress and to prevent it affecting your judgement and your physical or emotional capacity to undertake your caring role.

How stress affects your work

We have emphasised the importance of recognising the changes that can occur when you experience stress. It is very important to be aware of the implications of the changes caused by stress on your ability to fulfil your caring function. For example (referring back to the list on page 21):

- **Mental functioning:** if you are unable to absorb information, your concentration is not as good and your judgement is impaired. This may lead you to make an important error in your work.
- **Changes in emotions:** if you are feeling anxious, less confident than usual, or irritable, you will be less able to relate well and appropriately to the people you are caring for.
- **Changes in behaviour:** if you are having difficulty sleeping, finding it hard to manage your time, or drinking more alcohol, jobs will take longer to complete and you will become disorganised and unreliable.
- **Physical changes:** if you strain your back, suffer from headaches and migraines and succumb to colds and viruses, you will be off work sick and not fit and able to provide the care people need.

The manager's role

We have emphasised the need to be more aware of the changes that occur when stress is experienced. Not only does this involve monitoring your personal stress levels, there is also the need to keep an eye on stress levels in those you work with. As a manager it is particularly important to be watchful for signs of stress in your staff. Effective managers will keep a watch on stress levels whenever they allocate work, hold meetings with carers, or meet them individually in supervision. Remember that you only have access to the changes in someone's behaviour; you cannot know directly what someone is feeling unless they tell you. It is very easy to jump to the wrong conclusions when observing changes in others – the key is to use your observations and enquire about the person's well-being.

We have emphasised what happens when stress occurs, and the various changes that can show that stress is present. This is the first skill of managing stress. In the next chapter we go on to look at how stress can build up, and how the level of demand may become too much. This forms part of the second skill of managing stress – the ability to reduce unnecessary or inappropriate pressure.

KEY POINTS

- When stress occurs there will be a change in one or more area of functioning.
- The change can affect behaviour and mental, emotional or physical functioning.
- The particular pattern of change is personal and individual, so there is no checklist of symptoms.
- It is important to recognise when stress is happening at an early stage.
- It is helpful to use all available information to pick up when stress is happening.
- Feedback from other people is useful information.
- The activities in this book can help you to pick up your own patterns of response at different pressure levels.
- You can monitor yourself for any changes as they happen.
- The changes associated with your response to stress will affect your work.
- Managers have a key role in recognising when stress is occurring in their staff.

4 How pressure builds up

One of the main factors to take into account when thinking about managing stress is the level of pressure experienced. The other two factors are the level of resilience and the duration of the pressure, as we explored in Chapter 1. In this chapter we examine where the pressure comes from, and how it builds up.

There are three stages to working with the level of pressure in order to manage stress. These are:

1 *Identify the pressures that you are experiencing.*
2 *Distinguish between pressure which is necessary to do the task of caring and that which is not strictly necessary but creeps in anyway.*
3 *Reduce the level of unnecessary pressure.*

In this chapter we address the first two of those stages. We look at the third stage in Chapter 5.

Identifying the pressures of being a carer

CASE STUDY

Margaret is a woman in her late 40s. She has been working as a home carer for four years. She originally trained as a nurse, but decided to become a home carer as the hours fitted in with her family responsibilities. Margaret is a single parent with a son of 16 and a daughter of 12.

It has been a difficult week so far. Margaret's son has been getting into bad company, and coming in late. He is unresponsive to Margaret's attempts to talk with him. Her daughter has been withdrawing into her room and playing loud music. Margaret suspects that this is to avoid the tension in the household between Margaret and her son. On this particular morning, Margaret hears that a colleague is off sick, and she is asked to make an extra visit to a woman who needs help to get washed and dressed in the mornings. Margaret agrees to do this, and starts mentally juggling her timetable in her mind. She decides that if she cuts her visit short to Fred, a long-time service user she has befriended, she will be able to fit in the extra visit. She consoles herself by thinking that she can give Fred a little extra time next week. She knows how lonely Fred is and how much he appreciates having someone to talk to.

Margaret arrives at Fred's house early, already feeling pushed for time. She finds Fred in a happy state, as he has received some photographs of his grandchildren in Australia. He is very keen to show these to Margaret and wants to spend time talking about his family. Margaret cuts him short, tells him she cannot stay as long as usual, and then feels bad at the hurt look which crosses his face. She quickly follows it up by saying that she'll call in for a cup of tea next week. Fred cheers up at that offer but still appears unhappy that Margaret was not willing to listen to him that morning.

Margaret leaves Fred's later than she wanted, meets bad traffic, and arrives at the new person's house 20 minutes late. On arrival she is met with a barrage of complaints about why the usual home carer is not there. Mabel is less than pleased to see Margaret; she wants the familiarity of her usual person. She also complains because Margaret is late. With sinking heart Margaret explains the situation, and asks if there is anything she can get Mabel for breakfast. Mabel says she's 'gone past it' as Margaret was so late. Margaret is feeling impatient. It looks as if this visit is going to take longer than it should, which will make her even later for her next visit.

The day continues......

You may identify with elements of this scenario, or it may be something unfamiliar to you. You may have some feelings of sympathy for Margaret, or you may feel she is doing quite the wrong thing. We will now go through the case study and pull out the elements that lead to a build-up of pressure.

Pressure is the accumulation of all the demands experienced at any time. It is not one demand in itself that leads to stress; it is the way that the pressure adds up.

- Before Margaret had even started the day's work, she was feeling burdened by the demands of her home situation. Dealing with her two children was demanding in itself, and this depleted her resilience.
- On hearing of her colleague's absence, Margaret agreed to the extra visit. She was well aware that this would mean a tight schedule, but did not give herself the option of saying no to that request. The expectation that such requests will always be agreed to is a demand in itself.
- On arrival at Fred's house, Margaret felt that she did not have the time to respond to his request to look at the photos of his family. She did not want to upset him, and tried to compensate by offering to call round for a cup of tea.

This raises the whole issue of service users' expectations. The relationship between carer and service user is often a close one, and it is easy to slip into friendship. Fred was looking forward to seeing Margaret, and sharing his good news. She is an important part of his life. He has expectations of her over and above her professional carer role. It can be difficult to deal with these expectations. If Margaret feels that she has to respond to the expectations of people she helps professionally, that will be another demand. Margaret does seem pressured by Fred's demands, as she offers to call in for a cup of tea later in the week, thereby responding to his expectation of a relationship over and above the professional one.

- Margaret found it difficult to leave Fred, and so became even more behind schedule. It can be hard leaving when the person would rather you stayed for longer, and this is where the skill of assertion comes in (the next chapter looks, for example, at saying no). Being able to state your position clearly and directly is a key skill in withstanding pressure. Not being equipped with these skills leaves a person open to demands from others.

- On arrival at the new person's house, Margaret found herself unwelcome, and was on the receiving end of complaints. Dealing with aggressive behaviour, of which complaints are just one possible example, is a major demand and source of pressure.
- Mabel was feeling cross, and somewhat 'hard done by', and this had implications for Margaret's time management. Managing time to take account of what needs to be done in a way which is realistic is very demanding.

These are some of the demands that Margaret was facing:

- demands from her family;
- always saying yes to a request;
- meeting the expectations of service users;
- not being able to state her position clearly and directly;
- dealing with aggressive behaviour; and
- managing her time realistically.

These are only a sample of the possible demands that you can face as a carer. Some of the other demands that may be faced are:

- working in isolation without support;
- feeling vulnerable visiting areas with a reputation for robbery and assaults;
- feeling vulnerable making visits at night, even with protective equipment, alarms or a mobile phone;
- taking on the worries of the client;
- watching people deteriorate in health;
- not being valued; and
- needing to make decisions without reference to others.

There are three main areas where pressure can originate. These are:

- work-related stressors;
- personal stressors; and
- individual influences.

It is where these areas overlap, leading to the build-up of pressure, that problems occur.

Identifying the pressures you face

When undertaking a demanding role, such as that of a carer, it is easy to focus on the demands without really thinking about them. The first step to being able to do anything about the level of pressure is to take a moment to reflect on the demands and the pressures you face; to acknowledge that they are pressures.

ACTIVITY 5

We face a multitude of demands throughout our lives, so to make this activity more manageable we suggest that you consider just one day at a time.

Bring back to mind the last day on which you worked as a carer. Take each hour of that day in turn, and list the demands that you can remember experiencing in that hour. The table below may help you. Those hours you did not work may be left blank or you may wish to insert any other personal or family pressures, such as getting your children off to school.

Hour	Demands
7am	
8am	
9am	
10am	

Hour	Demands
11am	
12pm	
1pm	
2pm	
3pm	
4pm	
5pm	
6pm	
7pm	
8pm	
9pm	
10pm	

Now that you have listed the demands you were facing throughout that day, see if you can identify any patterns that emerge:

- Were there any times when the pressure was particularly high?
- What were the main demands you experienced?
- Is this a normal or unusual day; if unusual, in what way?
- Were any of these demands self-generated, ie ones you put on yourself?

Recognising different types of pressures

You may have been aware, either when reading the case study or when doing the exercise on identifying the pressures you face, that some of the demands made on you come from the world around you. These can take the form of requests from others, the expectations of others, bad traffic, or family demands, for example. However, you may well have noticed that some of the demands were ones you put on yourself.

The level of pressure we experience will inevitably be a mixture of demands from others and the outside world, and demands we generate in our own minds. Often it is easier to identify the demands others place on us, but these will only make up part of the whole picture.

The demands we place on ourselves are the result of years of experience, our early learning, and the decisions we have made about ourselves and how to cope with the world. Often they are so deeply embedded that we take them for granted, and may not even be aware that we are putting these demands on ourselves.

In the case of Margaret, one example of an internal pressure she placed on herself was the demand of not refusing the requests being made of her. She probably views this as part of her character and may well talk of herself as someone who always co-operates and responds positively to what others want of her. Others may well see her as someone who is helpful and someone who will always go out of her way to do what she can. The end result is that those around her may view her positively and also make extra demands on her, expecting that she will always agree. The other outcome is that she will often find herself overloaded. When overload happens it is likely to be her own needs that go unmet, while she struggles to do whatever she has agreed to, with little regard for herself.

Pressures we put on ourselves

There are some common pressures that are associated with the role of carer that we can put on ourselves:

- putting others first and ignoring yourself
- always getting everything right – the perfectionist streak
- stand on your own two feet – and never ask for help
- do everything quickly – whether speed is needed or not
- everything must be a struggle – and take a lot of effort

We will look at each of these pressure sources in turn, and invite you to see if any of them ring bells for you. We also start to look at the distinction between pressures which are necessary, and those which are not.

Putting others first and ignoring yourself

Being concerned about the needs of other people is an integral part of being a carer. It would be very difficult to provide care for someone if you had no thought or consideration for their needs. Showing and sharing that concern is an important part of care work, whatever the setting; there needs to be empathy and concern for the other person.

However, that is not the same as taking the view that it is only the needs of the other person that matter. It is not always easy to get a balance between your needs and those of the person you are providing care for. We will look at this skill in more detail in the next chapter. Here we want to emphasise the fine line between being concerned for the needs of the other person, and taking that concern to the point where you ignore your own needs and only consider those of the other person.

It is often said as high praise that a person is very caring. Often this means that they are selfless and do not think of themselves, and only think of others. The message that many women in particular learn as they are growing up is that care for others means not caring for yourself. Women learn from childhood that they are expected to be the carers in their family, often to the detriment of their own needs and aspirations. This is an unnecessary pressure. It is possible to take account both of other people and of yourself.

Always getting everything right – the perfectionist streak

Most people take pride in doing a good job. Doing a good job is an important part of feeling that you are making a contribution, and are of value. Doing what is necessary to do your tasks well as a carer or a manager is a necessary demand.

However, the demand to do a good job can be taken to extremes. An unnecessary pressure is when the demand to do a good job moves into the demand for perfection. A very strong internal pressure is the demand to get everything absolutely right, with no mistakes ever being allowed. We are not arguing that mistakes are a good thing. In the context of the provision of personal care, mistakes can often be costly in human terms as well as financially. We argue that mistakes should be avoided wherever possible, and you should learn from them when they happen – an important 'message' for managers. However, for someone who places a demand on themselves to always get everything right at all costs, making a mistake can mean they are very hard on themselves.

Forgetting to make a visit is a serious error, and one which warrants corrective action. Taking the wrong turning on the way to a visit is hardly grounds for castigation in your own mind as someone who can't get anything right. We may be exaggerating, but we have come across many people who are driven by a need for perfection, and who really do feel like failures because they are not able to reach their aim; perfection every time. Striving to do a good job is a necessary pressure, whereas striving for perfection is an unnecessary pressure as perfection is unobtainable.

Stand on your own two feet – and never ask for help

There is a very strong wish in a lot of people to stand on their own two feet and be independent. Independence is a state which is often held up as being desirable. The opposite is usually cited as dependence. We would totally support the wish to be independent, but, again, sometimes this can be taken too far. It is more than just being independent if it is impossible to ever ask for help, or say there is a problem. The internal demand to always get things done on your own, and to see it as a sign of weakness to ask for help, adds to the pressure level and, when others, like managers, are there to help, may needlessly exaggerate those pressures.

Asking for help and support when appropriate is a very useful skill in managing pressure, but one that is difficult to access if the demand inside yourself requires total independence. This is the internal demand which insists that a smiling, coping face is always presented to the world. When asked how things are, the response is always 'fine'.

Do everything quickly – whether speed is needed or not

This version of internal pressure requires that everything has to be done at top speed and life is led at a hurried pace from morning till night. It is often associated with an unrealistic assessment of how long a task will actually take. The relationship with time is seen as one of beating the clock, and trying to get more and more done at a faster and faster pace.

There are tasks which need to be done quickly, and where speed is essential, but there are also tasks which improve from taking a little more time and care. When the internal demand is to do everything at a fast rate, the distinction between tasks requiring time, and tasks requiring speed, is not made and everything is tackled quickly. It is as if there are rewards to be gained from completing things in record time; this is one sure way of creating unnecessary pressure.

Everything must be a struggle – and take a lot of effort

In this version of demand from within, the key message is that every task must require a lot of effort. It is reminiscent of old school reports

which stated 'could try harder'. It is the effort which is seen as important, whether or not the task requires it. It is as if effort brings its own
reward, whatever the outcome. 'At least I tried hard' is the statement
made by people who feel driven to put a lot into everything they do.

There are obviously jobs which do require a lot of effort: equally,
there are some which do not require great exertion, and which may
even benefit from a more relaxed approach. Deciding which jobs
require effort, and which do not, will not be easy for the person who
is driven by effort. It is the inability to make the decision about what
is appropriate for the task in hand which leads to this internal demand
creating unnecessary pressure.

These are five of the most common ways in which we can put unnecessary pressure on ourselves. These will add to the pressures already
experienced from the world, so that it is possible to see how they can
all add up to a higher than optimum pressure level.

Making the distinction between necessary and unnecessary pressure

When looking at the level of pressure as the first component of managing stress, the first task is to identify where the pressures are coming
from. The second is to grapple with the distinction between demands
which are necessary, and those which are not.

By 'necessary pressures' we mean ones which are inherent in carrying
out your role. There are many necessary demands which go with the
carer's role. Carers need to:

- be responsive to what individuals want and need;
- treat everyone they care for with dignity;
- keep to appointments;
- perform to a satisfactory and appropriate level of competence; and
- ensure that they are skilled and equipped to do their job – a responsibility shared with their line manager.

These 'pressures' are a necessary part of doing the caring task and
doing it well. We all need an optimum level of pressure, and these
demands on their own should not be excessive.

When coming into the role for the first time, there will be the additional pressures created by the novelty and unfamiliarity of the situation, but with time, and as your skills increase, the demands of unfamiliarity will decrease.

There are many pressures which are not an integral part of doing the caring role well. We have outlined some of the ways in which we can put unnecessary pressure on ourselves. The next step is to consider the demands and pressures you have identified for yourself, and see what are necessary pressures and identify those which are unnecessary.

We suggest that you now revisit the list of pressures you identified for yourself in Activity 5 (on pages 32–33), and see which of those are an integral and necessary part of your role, and which are not. You may find this easy to do, or the distinction may not be so clear-cut. We suggest that you bear the distinction in mind, as the second key skill of managing stress is the ability to reduce unnecessary pressure. In order to do that, it helps to be able to identify unnecessary pressures.

Implications for managers

Undertaking responsibility for managing the work of others brings its own demands; managers, just like care staff, need time to reflect on the build-up of pressures for themselves.

When it comes to getting the best out of staff, having information about the level of pressure faced by staff at any given time is a vital part of the information needed to manage well. We are not suggesting that managers take an intrusive interest in the personal lives of staff, only that it is helpful to have some knowledge of pressure points for staff outside of the work environment.

We have looked in this chapter at how the pressure level can build up and at some of the sources of pressure. In particular, we have made the distinction between pressures which come from others and those which we generate ourselves. We have emphasised the importance of identifying pressures which are necessary, and those which are not. In the next chapter, we continue to look at skills which help reduce unnecessary pressure.

KEY POINTS

- There are different types of pressures.
- We can put pressure on ourselves as well as experiencing demands from others.
- Putting others first and ignoring our own needs is a source of pressure.
- Striving for perfection adds extra pressure.
- Aiming to be independent and never asking for help increases the pressure level, especially when help is available.
- Doing everything at top speed, whether necessary or not, is a demand.
- Putting a great deal of effort into a task, whether it warrants it or not, increases demand.
- We face some pressures which are a necessary part of the carer role.
- We also face some pressures which are unnecessary.
- Making the distinction between necessary and unnecessary pressure is helpful.

5 The skills of reducing unnecessary pressure

We have looked at attitudes to stress and recognising it. In this chapter we move on to look at the skills of managing stress by reducing unnecessary pressure. This links back to our original model of the three factors that together add up to determine the pressure level. One key factor is the level of pressure, which is made up of necessary pressure and elements of unnecessary pressure. In this chapter we look at the unnecessary pressure that we can sometimes face, and how it is possible to reduce it to make the stress equation more balanced.

The benefits of skills for managing pressure levels

When faced with an overwhelming set of demands, people often wish that these pressures would simply go away. It is the mountain of pressure that leads to the feelings of stress. If this mountain would only get a little smaller, life would be more manageable.

The next step is to turn to those people who you view as placing the demands on you and wish that they would stop causing you stress. The question that you may be tempted to ask yourself is: 'Why don't they, whoever they are, stop doing this or that, or make fewer demands on me?'

It is only a small step from wishing that other people would be less demanding to blaming them, and feeling resentful at the amount of pressure they put on you. When stress is beginning to mount up, feeling resentful at the demands others are placing on you simply adds to your pressure.

It is tempting to have a moan about how demanding other people are, and whilst gossip is always something we need to keep in check, the odd moan can relieve some tensions. Or you may think that if only 'they' stopped making demands on you, everything would be all right; but the most constructive step is to learn the skills of reducing unnecessary pressure.

Learning the skills of how to reduce unnecessary pressure helps in a couple of ways, both of which go a long way to moving your stress balance in the right direction.

By acquiring the skills of reducing unnecessary pressure, you know there will always be some techniques 'up your sleeve' for managing the pressure level. It doesn't help when the pressure level mounts, and you don't feel there is any way you can deal with it. Then it just feels as if the world is overwhelming, and you are powerless. Learning and using skills of reducing unnecessary pressure immediately gives you a sense of having some say in the amount of pressure you face. When you have these skills at your disposal, you are in a position to do something about the demands you are facing – other than just suffering them.

As you become more familiar and at ease with using the skills of reducing unnecessary pressure, this will in itself increase your resilience.

Resilience is the second component of the stress equation. Stress is not just caused by the level of pressure alone. It is the balance between the level of pressure and the level of resilience which will determine whether you feel on top of the world, or at your wits' end, and barely capable of coping properly. Feeling helpless in the face of ever-mounting pressure is a sure recipe for stress. Feeling equipped with some skills which will reduce the pressure level is a way of managing stress.

We will look in more detail in the next chapter at further ways of increasing your resilience level. The point that we want to emphasise here is that learning the skills of reducing pressure will increase your feelings of resilience as well anyway.

Three key skills

In the previous chapter we invited you to reflect on the demands you face, and to make the distinction between those pressures which are necessary and those which are unnecessary. Remember that we all need a certain level of pressure and stimulation in order to function at our best. Not only will necessary pressures come with the role of carer, but they will also be needed to keep us alert and working well. It is the unnecessary pressures which warrant attention.

Three key skills in reducing unnecessary pressure are:

- **being able to refuse requests and say no assertively;**
- **expressing your wants and needs clearly and assertively; and**
- **setting clear boundaries around your role as a carer.**

In Chapter 4 we used the example of Margaret and took a brief glimpse into a day in her life to get a feel for some of the demands she was facing. We can link the unnecessary pressures placed on her to the three key skills:

- Early in her day Margaret was asked if she would fit in an extra visit. She doesn't allow herself to refuse requests, so she automatically agreed. Fitting in extra work at short notice is often necessary but the decision does need to be realistic, based upon an assessment of competing demands. This will not be possible unless there is the option to refuse. She needs to learn to say no.
- Later in the day when making her first visit, Margaret had difficulty telling Fred that she was pushed for time and could not sit and look at his family photos. She needs to learn to express her own wants and needs assertively.
- Margaret felt guilty that she could not stay and chat with Fred, and, to ease her feelings of guilt, she offered to call round in her own time for a cup of tea. Margaret already faced pressures at home from her children, which suggests that making yet another commitment might not be a good idea. She needs to learn to set clear boundaries around her role as a carer.

These three form the backbone of the skills you need for reducing unnecessary pressure. We will look at them in detail. However we first need to introduce a mechanism which is central to the way we can create pressure for ourselves, and which is also central to the way in which we can reduce it. This is the 'internal dialogue'.

The internal dialogue

The internal dialogue is a part of us which accompanies us in everything we do, and which is rarely acknowledged publicly. It is the conversation we have running in our heads all the time. We do not need another person present for us to be involved in, at times, a lengthy debate. We can do that in our own minds, all by ourselves. The notion of talking to ourselves is one which has had a bad press over the years. It has been said that talking to yourself is the 'first sign of madness', and that hearing voices is a very bizarre phenomenon. The internal dialogue is not usually conducted out loud. Rather it is a conversation that goes on quietly in our own minds, between different parts of ourselves. It has been described as like having the radio on low. We do not always tune in to what is being said, but the voices are going on in the background nonetheless.

The internal dialogue plays a very important role in creating pressure. Remember that it is not the events which happen to us which cause the pressure, it is the way in which we respond to those events.

When we described the fight/flight response, we were identifying a very quick response to something which posed a threat to our well-being. The ability to get out of the way or to destroy the opposition is a necessary survival skill when faced with something dangerous. Though nowadays we do not face large dangerous beasts, we sometimes respond as if we do. We do not literally face a woolly mammoth, but when the internal dialogue tells us that the difficult person making unreasonable demands on us is really just the same as a mammoth, then a mammoth is what we perceive. When information comes in through our senses, we have to interpret it, and this is where the internal dialogue comes in.

For example, if we are in a strange neighbourhood at night and that area is known for assaults, our internal dialogue is primed to perceive danger.

As we drive to the late-night visit, the internal dialogue might be going something like this: *'This is a dodgy area; it is only last week that someone was attacked here. I am here on my own and therefore I am likely to be attacked.'* If a dark shape emerges from the shadows, it is not surprising that the heart starts to race and all our nerves are on edge.

Thus the internal dialogue plays a very important role in how we perceive or interpret events. It also plays a key role in how we look ahead and foresee what is about to happen. This can either create additional pressure, or act to calm us down.

Let's go back to the example of Margaret. As she drove to make her visit to Fred, there could have been a number of internal dialogues running in her head. One dialogue could have gone:

'Oh dear, I have not got so much time to spend with Fred today, I do hope that he will not mind. I do feel bad when I can't give him as much attention as he would like.'

Alternatively, her dialogue might have been:

'I do not have much time to get everything done at Fred's today. I do hope that he behaves himself and is not awkward and demanding. I do hate it when he whines at me, I feel like walking out and not coming back, he is such a nuisance.'

This second dialogue is unlikely, given what we already know about Margaret. The internal dialogue we run as we approach an encounter will affect how we engage in that encounter. The internal dialogue has an important role to play in making the future real.

The creativity of the internal dialogue can lead us to worry unnecessarily. Worry has been described as anticipatory stress – the way in which we anticipate what is about to happen and expect that it is bound to be bad. As human beings we have an amazing ability to foresee dire events. Particularly in the absence of information, we tend to fear the worst. Perhaps it was to counter that fear that the phrase 'no news is good news' was first invented. It does not come easily to expect good news when there is no information forthcoming. The internal dialogue is the mechanism which determines whether we worry or not.

Not only does the internal dialogue play an important role in getting to grips with the future, it also plays an important role in making sense of the past. If you have had a difficult visit, you may find yourself replaying that visit in your mind as you drive away. You may try to make sense of what happened, or you may reflect on how you handled it, or you may look for an excuse to give yourself a hard time. Reflecting on our past actions can be a very good opportunity for learning, but, equally, it can be a good opportunity for reinforcing something negative in the way we see ourselves. However it is used, that companion conversation in our own mind plays a key role in our understanding of past events, as well as in the ways we interpret the here and now.

So the internal dialogue plays a part in how we perceive events, how we look ahead to the future and the sense we make of the past. The final role it plays is to store our unwritten rules, a key element when it comes to the skills of reducing unnecessary pressure.

Rewriting our unwritten rules

Each of us has a unique past. Our own particular upbringing left us with a set of unwritten rules about how the world is and about how we have to behave in it. We have already seen how these unwritten rules can create additional pressure when we looked at the five common sets of belief which drive behaviour. To recap, the ones we looked at were the need to:

- do everything perfectly;
- do it all on your own;
- always put others first;
- do everything really quickly; and
- put a lot of effort into your work.

These are five common sets of unwritten rules, but we end up believing them as fact, rather than as beliefs held in our internal dialogue.

Thinking back to Margaret, there were some clues about the unwritten rules in her internal dialogue. For example: *'It is not OK to refuse a request; if someone asks you to do something, you must always do it.'*

If this is an unwritten rule which has been lodged in Margaret's internal dialogue for many years, it is not surprising that the belief affects her behaviour. Often we do not know what is stored in our internal dialogue. We have been used to acting in a particular way, perhaps for years and have lost track of the fact that our behaviour is based on our own personal set of unwritten rules.

Let's pause a moment and think where you need to go from here. What you've learned is that:

- You need some techniques 'up your sleeve' for managing pressure levels.
- It is the balance between pressure levels and your own personal 'resilience' that determines how good you're feeling.
- Feeling helpless in the face of ever-mounting pressure is a sure recipe for stress.
- There are three skills that help reduce unnecessary pressure:

  – learning to say no;
  – learning to express yourself clearly; and
  – setting clear boundaries.

To develop those three skills effectively, there are three separate steps you need to take:

- Identify the unwritten rules in your internal dialogue.
- Learn to question your unwritten rules.
- Learn to substitute more helpful permissions to yourself.

Learning to say no

Learning to refuse requests made by others is a vital skill in managing pressure levels, but one that poses problems for many of us, particularly women. For many people, saying no is seemingly just not part of their vocabulary or repertoire. If the permission to refuse requests is not part of your internal dialogue, every request that is made of you is agreed, leading to overload within a short space of time.

Now let's use each of the three steps to see if they can help us move from an unhelpful position to a more helpful one when it comes to saying no.

The first step is **to be aware of what is currently stored in your internal dialogue** regarding refusing requests. This will vary from person to person. You are looking to see what it is you are carrying around with you – the 'messages' that either hinder you or give you permission to say no.

Once you have identified what your particular messages are, then you can move on to the next step, which is **questioning your internal dialogue**. We are suggesting that the ability to say no is a useful skill to have. We want you to be on the lookout for any messages which hinder you refusing requests and saying no. If you can identify any elements of your internal dialogue which get in the way of you feeling at ease saying no, these could do with some questioning.

By questioning your internal dialogue, we do not want you to berate yourself for the fact that you have not got it all right yet – after all, how many of us have? We want you simply to ask yourself if the belief which you stored away in your internal dialogue many years ago, still holds true today or whether it could do with a rethink. For example, a very common reason why many people find if difficult to refuse a request is the belief that they must always do what other people want of them, regardless of whether they want to do it or not. This might be described as 'it would be rude to refuse', 'I don't want to upset them', or 'it is far more important than anything I had planned'. There are endless versions of the internal dialogue which stop us saying no. The trick is to take each part in turn and to question it.

In the examples given above, questioning it would mean saying gently to yourself:

'If I refused to do that now, would it really be so rude or inappropriate of me? I had better pay attention to how I put things, but would saying no be so rude after all?'

The final stage is **substituting something more likely to encourage saying no**. Continuing the example given above, this might be something like:

'It is OK to say no, if I am unable or unwilling to do what it is that is asked of me, as long as I do it in a way which is not rude or

aggressive to the person making the request, or gives the impression that I'm refusing a reasonable instruction.'

This is a perfectly good basis for saying no, and takes into account the fact that few people like being rude.

ACTIVITY 6

Think of a situation where you wanted to say no, but the words just didn't come out right for you. How could you have put things differently? Use the space below for your answers.

Expressing yourself clearly

To say no, you need to know what you want and need. The first step towards a clear expression of your wants and needs is to give yourself permission to *have* your own wants. This is not as surprising as it seems. We have often come across people in care work who appear to deny that they have any wants or needs of their own. This denial can be linked to the belief that other people's needs must always come first, but, even then, that is not quite the same thing as denying your own needs.

It can be perceived as a sign of someone coping well that they do not have needs of their own. For example in one particular situation we have encountered, the home carer dealt with the negative feelings she had about a difficult service user indirectly. She was really worried about maintaining her image as a person who could cope in all situations and therefore did not give herself permission to express herself clearly and directly. Instead she expressed her feeling in the log or daily record kept in the service user's home. This inevitably had serious consequences as it was read by others.

We find the denial of personal needs worrying. A skill which goes beyond expressing your wants and needs clearly is taking steps to get them met. We look at this further in the next chapter. Here we want to emphasise that it is difficult to express your wants and needs clearly if you do not allow yourself to have any.

Let us go back to the example of Margaret and her reluctance to tell Fred that she was only able to stay for a short time. She was not denying the reality of the situation, that she needed to go shortly, so she was not denying her needs; she was just having some difficulty expressing them.

Once you allow yourself to have wants and needs, the next stage is to see if there is anything in your internal dialogue which might be getting in the way of telling others what you want and need.

There are a whole range of different possibilities which can hinder expression. These can include:

- *'This person is hard of hearing; they would not hear anyway.'*
- *'This person never listens to a word I say, so there is no point in saying anything, they will not listen anyway.'*
- *'My family never listens to a word I say, so this person will not either.'*
- *'It is kinder not to mention it and then just leave; it would only upset them to know I was going quickly.'*

The important thing is to identify exactly what it is in your internal dialogue which holds you back from expressing yourself clearly. The more specific you can be when you identify what's holding you back, the more chance there will be of removing this barrier.

Once you've started to question your internal dialogue, keep the flow of questions coming gently. Put new dialogues in place if they are needed. What you're learning, all the time, is that it is possible to express yourself clearly.

Setting clear boundaries

This skill is one which is easy to talk about, yet hard for many people to put into practice.

ACTIVITY 7

Let's think for a moment about why setting boundaries can be so difficult. Here are two questions to start you off considering this. Try to answer yes or no to each of them.

Q Can I clearly separate the roles of carer and friend?

Y ☐   N ☐

Q If you are a family carer, do you find time for yourself?

Y ☐   N ☐

If you answered 'no' to either question, or even if you hesitated a moment with your answer, this paragraph will help you. **In order to set clear boundaries for yourself, you need to have a very clear sense of who you are**. If you do not have a clear sense of who you are, and tend to be swayed by how others want you to be, then it will be more difficult to set boundaries with other people.

We saw in the example with Margaret that she overcame her negative feelings at having to leave Fred quickly by offering to call round in her own time for a cup of tea. This may reflect Margaret's friendly nature and kind heart, but it also blurs the boundary between her role as carer and becoming a friend. That boundary needs very careful handling.

Providing care for someone does not mean that you are available to them 24 hours a day, 7 days a week. If you are a family carer, then it may feel as if there is no getting away from your caring responsibilities; your time needs careful managing to give yourself some respite. When you are a paid carer, then the boundaries are much clearer, and it is then simply a question of getting your internal dialogue in line with maintaining those boundaries. Margaret was juggling at least two roles – her role as carer and her role as single parent. Each of these roles come with their own sets of demands, and it will make things harder to manage if the boundaries are unclear.

Planning to put these skills into practice

Now we come to the final step in this stage of our learning. Let's remind ourselves of the skills we have already understood in order to reduce those unnecessary pressures we identified for ourselves:

- learning to say no;
- expressing wants and needs clearly; and
- setting clear boundaries.

If the first step in learning to use those skills is to recognise the importance of the internal dialogue and the second step is giving yourself permission to use those skills, then the final step is actually putting them into practice.

Even when the internal dialogue has been duly examined, questioned and helpful permissions put into place, there can still be the nagging question: 'Well, how do I actually do it?'

There are two general principles that underpin putting these skills into practice.

The first principle is to be aware of both your verbal and non-verbal behaviour. When communicating with others we give messages both through what we say and also by what we do (like gestures, facial expressions, or the way we dress). Both forms of communication need attention when planning to give a clear message.

The second principle is to use words and actions which treat the other person positively and with dignity. This is a value which underpins all caring work, but when dealing with a difficult issue such as stating your own needs, it is possible for the odd aggressive word or tone to slip in. When dealing with difficult things, such as facing a lifelong reluctance to say no, or setting clear boundaries when this has not been your past pattern, then words and gestures we do not usually use may 'pop' in to our conversation. What we then find is that the person we are talking to 'homes in' on that aggressive word or tone, and doesn't hear what we want to tell them about our needs, wants or boundaries.

The three activities below will help you say difficult things without getting into trouble.

ACTIVITY 8

Learning to say no

You need to hear yourself say the actual word 'no'. This may not have been allowed in your upbringing, and may not be part of your vocabulary now, so hearing yourself say it is unfamiliar.

1 Find a friend or colleague to help you with this exercise.

2 Ask your partner in this exercise to think of five questions to ask you which are not about important matters, preferably about quite trivial and even humorous things, to which you can answer no. In using this exercise we have found questions such as 'Will you lend me £2 million?', 'Will you stand on your head in the corner?' and 'Will you do my job for me?' to be quite useful.

3 Then find a quiet place and give your attention to the questions you are going to be asked. Your partner in the exercise then asks you the questions and you reply with a simple 'no'. Pause for a moment after each question and reflect on what it feels like to actually say no.

4 At the end of the series of questions, discuss what it was like for you saying no and what your partner heard and observed.

5 Then change places and give yourself the opportunity of hearing someone say no to your questions. Discuss what it was like for you when someone said no. Was it really so terrible? Did it feel so hurtful? You may discover that it is not so bad after all. Move on to saying 'no' about something that relates to your work.

With this exercise the questions are unimportant and even trivial. Gradually find opportunities to practise saying no, even when it is an important issue.

ACTIVITY 9

Expressing your wants

This is another exercise which will be more effective if you can find someone willing to do it with you. Find a quiet place again, and explain to your partner that what you want them to do is listen to you expressing your wants clearly.

1 Take a few moments to focus your mind. Think back to your last birthday and tell your partner what it was that you really wanted for a present.

2 Then focus ahead and tell your partner what you want to do for your next holiday.

3 Pause and reflect on what it was like to talk about what you have wanted in the past and what you want in the future. Often it is easier to allow yourself to want in the past and the future and not so easy to express what you want right now.

4 Then take a few moments, close your eyes, take a few deep breaths and see what comes to mind about what you want right at that moment. It is fine if it is something small or trivial; just express it to your partner using the words 'I want'. Then take a few moments to discuss it.

5 The final stage is to reverse the exercise and ask your partner to express their wants, in the past, in the future, and in the present. Be aware of your response to hearing someone else tell you of their wants. You may find that it is actually something which draws you together and is good to hear.

ACTIVITY *10*

Setting boundaries

Learning to set boundaries is not always easy as it is quite an intangible thing to do. To create a good foundation, we will use the notion of 'visualisation'.

1 Find a quiet place and take a few moments on your own to relax and gather your thoughts.

2 Focus on being a carer and what that means for you.

3 Think of all the tasks that are involved in your care work and put each task in a brightly coloured box in your mind.

4 When each task that you can think of to do with being a carer is in its own box, put all the boxes in a big pile.

5 When the boxes are in a pile, draw a coloured rope around the whole pile.

6 Take a mental step back, and notice the boundary you have drawn around your care work tasks.

You may find it difficult to step back, but this exercise will encourage you to use your own, vivid powers of creativity to start setting clear boundaries. Whenever you need to set a boundary, the image of brightly coloured rope can be helpful.

Increasing resilience further

In this chapter we have identified three key skills which will stand you in good stead to manage unnecessary pressure. These skills will also help you to feel that you do have options in the face of demands, which in itself will help increase your resilience level. If you are a manager, the more you are able to identify triggers for unnecessary pressure in your staff and help them avoid them, the more effective staff you will have.

In the next chapter we go on to look at how you can increase your resilience further in order to equip you to deal with pressure more effectively.

KEY POINTS

- Unnecessary pressure can come from the way we respond to events.
- Our response to events is influenced by the conversation we all have with ourselves, which is called the 'internal dialogue'.
- The internal dialogue influences our behaviour.
- We act as if to a set of unwritten rules.
- Challenging our set of unwritten rules is a useful skill.
- There are three skills which particularly help in reducing unnecessary pressure.
- Learning to refuse requests and say no is a helpful skill.
- Learning to state your own needs and wants clearly is useful.
- Learning to set boundaries (lines over which you will not go) is helpful.
- Practising these three skills will reduce unnecessary pressure and also add to your resilience level.

6 Increasing your level of resilience

In the previous chapter we focused on three skills which are helpful in managing the level of demand and reducing unnecessary pressure. Learning these skills and using them will also help to increase your resilience by giving you a feeling of control over some of the demands you face. In this chapter we will look at three further ways in which you can increase your resilience and become more able to deal with demands. These three areas are:

- *ensuring that you get the support you need in your role as a carer;*
- *clarifying your training needs with others and becoming more skilled; and*
- *getting balance in your life – ensuring that you have 'stability zones'.*

The messages in this chapter are also very important for managers because of their role in supporting, monitoring, developing and supervising staff.

Giving yourself permission to take care of yourself

Before we look at these three strategies for increasing resilience in more detail, we need to revisit the internal dialogue once again. This is to ensure that the conversation you are having with yourself really will allow you to build up your resilience.

Whatever the particular strategy you adopt to increase your level of resilience, the one essential which has to be in place is a belief in the importance of taking care of yourself. This is not always easy to do when you spend your time providing care for others.

As we pointed out earlier in the book, two of the major components which add up to determine your stress level are the level of pressure you are experiencing, and your level of resilience. We looked in Chapter 5 at how you can reduce demand by using the skills of saying no; expressing your wishes clearly; and setting boundaries. It is often thought that reducing or resisting pressure is the only way in which you can manage stress. Yet how resilient you are feeling at any point in time will determine your ability to respond to the pressure. If your resilience is good, you will find that you are able to withstand a greater level of pressure with comfort. If your resilience is low, you will experience stress sooner.

Resilience is not something that is fixed, either at birth or by education or upbringing. The level of resilience you have at any one time will vary. The level will certainly be influenced by all your experiences in the past, but despite, or perhaps because of, these experiences, **your level of resilience can be increased**. Working to increase your level of resilience takes time, effort, and, importantly, a belief that working on yourself in this way is a worthwhile thing to do.

If you spend a high proportion of your time providing care for others it is tempting to think of care as something which is only needed by those you care for. It is easy to slip into thinking of yourself, the carer, as someone who does not have needs for care. After all, the internal dialogue can run, 'care is what your clients need'.

We recognise that there are few people who really do make such a clear-cut distinction between carer and cared for. Yet there can be traces of such thinking in the internal dialogue. If that is the case, it will not be easy to pay attention to what is needed to increase your level of resilience, as that involves recognising your own needs and taking care of yourself.

ACTIVITY 11

How easy do you find it to take care of yourself?

It is not always easy to devote effort to looking after ourselves because we can carry round values and beliefs that tell us that doing this is wrong.

Read through the following statements and mark whether you agree or disagree with each one. Even if it is hard, try to give a definite answer one way or the other. Remember that the object of this exercise is to help you take care of *yourself*.

Statement	Agree	Disagree
1 It is always better to spend my time on others rather than on myself	■	☐
2 Looking after myself is sensible	☐	■
3 What I want or need for myself is less important than what others want from me	■	☐
4 I am important and my needs are important	☐	■
5 Looking after myself is selfish	■	☐
6 I deserve attention from myself	☐	■
7 I am not worth spending time on and looking after	■	☐
8 I must look after myself, because only then am I in a fit state to look after other people	☐	■

9   No grown person should need looking after; only children need looking after

10   Other people matter but so do I

11   Other people matter more than I do

12   Everybody needs looking after, whatever their age

13   If I do require some care and attention, I will have to fight for it

14   If I need some care and attention, it is up to me to be assertive in asking for what I need

Scoring

Give yourself a score of 3 points for each time you have placed a tick in an *unshaded* box.

The maximum score is 42.

If you scored between 30 and 42 – you have a set of beliefs and values which will help you in taking care of yourself. You are unlikely to have much difficulty developing a strategy to look after yourself.

If you scored between 21 and 30 – you have some views which could get in the way of your care of yourself. You may need to re-evaluate these before you can plan an effective strategy.

If you scored less than 21 – it is likely that you will find it hard to plan a programme for looking after yourself, because your attitudes do not predispose you to take care of yourself. The values and beliefs you hold will get in the way of devising a constructive strategy. You will help yourself if you can develop a more positive view of the need to take care of yourself.

Now that you have checked that your internal dialogue is helpful to the idea of taking care of yourself and increasing your resilience, we will move on to examine three particular strategies which can help.

Getting support in your role as carer

Caring is often an isolated occupation. This can be the case even if you work in a residential home. The caring that you do may be shared with the service user only, or with one or two of your colleague care workers; whatever the situation, the actual interaction between you and the person you care for usually happens in private, away from other people. Some of your time will be spent in various interactions where you are providing care as the sole carer. There is no immediate support for you in that role when you are interacting with service users.

What support can give you

There will be many events which occur during the course of your caring which can raise questions in your mind or even cause you to doubt whether you did the right thing. If your time is spent going from one relatively short period with one person, straight on to the next, there is little opportunity to resolve your doubts and anxieties.

Equally, the conversations and interactions you have with those you care for may leave you with unresolved feelings. Again, if you are going straight from one encounter to the next, there will be little time to deal with these feelings, and they will simply stay with you through the day.

Getting support in your role as a carer means at the very least having an opportunity, in a non-judgemental setting, to:

- spend time with others who know and understand the carer's role;
- share your concerns;
- raise questions;
- deal with unresolved feelings; and
- generally debrief on your work.

ACTIVITY *12*

Where your support comes from now

Reflect back on the past seven days and identify, for each day, who provided the support, and where and how it was provided.

Day	Who provided support?	Where was it provided?	How was it provided?
Monday			
Tuesday			
Wednesday			
Thursday			
Friday			
Saturday			
Sunday			

Looking back on the week, we invite you to consider and reflect on the following questions:

- Was the level of support enough for you?

- Who were your main sources of support? Did this include your line manager? Could they play a stronger role in supporting you?

- Was the support you received offered to you or did you ask for it?

Ensuring that you get the support which you need at the time *you* need it means that the ability to ask for support is crucial.

Asking for support

Even if you recognise the need for support, you may not feel comfortable asking for it. Sometimes there is a part of the internal dialogue which goes something like this:

'If they cared about me they would notice and offer support without me having to say anything. If I have to ask for support it is because 'they' are insensitive or unobservant.'

If you're inclined to think that other people are 'insensitive and unobservant', what the internal dialogue might be telling you deep down inside is something like:

'No-one stops to take any notice of me. I'm just not worth it.'

Remember what this book has taught you about your own worth. You personally have considerable worth. We wish to encourage you to believe that you deserve the support you rightly need in your demanding role as a carer.

However no-one else can be as clear about the support you need as you can be yourself. While care service managers should always be sensitive to the needs of their staff, even your line manager cannot be a mind-reader. Your own internal dialogue can inhibit asking for support. Try finding the courage to say things as they are for *you*.

Being able to ask for support when you need it is a very good way of increasing your resilience and taking good care of yourself. We recognise that it is not always easy, and therefore suggest that you practice asking for support. This means asking not just once, but several times, especially if you know that asking for support is something you struggle with.

Getting the training you need and increasing your skill levels

A key part of good resilience is to have a sense of your own competence. This is where training and development comes in.

Development and competence

The clearer the idea you have of your skills and abilities, the more resilient you will be in the face of pressure.

To illustrate this, imagine that Margaret, in the case study, was an inexperienced carer who hadn't had the opportunity to weigh up what she could or couldn't do. If she had been asked to fit in an extra visit at short notice, this may well have led to her worrying in her internal dialogue about whether she would be required to undertake any new tasks or activities. This could raise doubts about whether she would be competent. Often worrying about the future is based on worrying about whether you have the competence necessary to face the unknown.

Having a sense of competence is reassuring. This is one reason why change can often be threatening, because a different scenario brings with it demands for different skills. We can comfort ourselves that we have the skills and abilities to cope with the present situation; we are aware of our competence. But change the situation and suddenly our current skills may not be good enough, may not equip us to cope.

Development as a lifelong event

This leads to the second key point related to training and development. Training and development is an excellent way of upgrading your skills and learning new competences. Viewing development as an ongoing process will keep attention constantly on your resilience level.

Training and development is sometimes seen as the same as education – do it when you are young, get your qualifications and that is that. We are suggesting that development, focusing on acquiring new skills and developing existing abilities, is not a one-off process.

The requirements of providing care are changing as the context in which care is provided changes. The role of carer has evolved beyond recognition over the past few years. The organisational context in which care is provided has also been transformed. So it is not possible to predict all the wide range of skills which are going to be needed in the future as a carer. These changes highlight the need to consider personal development as a career-long process.

It is sometimes tempting to think of development as consisting solely of training courses. There are many excellent courses available and the organisation which employs you will have its own views on training and may have a well-developed training programme for carers. However, developing your skills needs to be an ongoing process in a wide range of situations including, for example, inducting a new member of staff, group discussions, annual performance appraisal, supervision and, as we have said, opportunities for reflection after a stressful situation.

Whatever your organisation's approach, it is important that you identify your own development and training needs, ask for what you want, and increase your competence and thereby confidence in your role as a carer.

Development and confidence

Confidence, like a sense of competence, is a very important and strong factor for building resilience. Yet it is intangible and hard to pin down. Confident people can seem to have an armour against stress, whereas when confidence is lacking, demands can easily become overwhelming.

There is a two-way relationship between development and confidence. An essential element of confidence is knowledge of yourself. If you do not know yourself very well, it is difficult to be confident about an unknown quantity. Spending time in development activities, such as reading this book, helps to increase your knowledge of yourself, which in turn increases confidence.

Confidence is not the same as arrogance. In our view, arrogance is an unwarranted sense of your good points, with little or no recognition of any less than good points. It is an unbalanced view because every person is a mixture of good and less good points; that is in the nature of being human. It is equally unbalanced to focus simply on your bad points, and not give recognition of your good ones. This will not lead to confidence, but to an overwhelming sense of your weaknesses.

We see confidence as the ability to acknowledge your good and bad points and to feel comfortable with both. Supervision at work should help you with this. If there are any aspects of yourself that you are not comfortable with, that is a starting point for development.

Therefore, to be really effective, a personalised training and development programme, which takes your training needs into account, has to be based on a knowledge and assessment of your weaker areas. It takes confidence, and sometimes help, to acknowledge your weaker points. It is an unconfident person who insists that they have no weak areas. Whatever it feels like to be on the receiving end of arrogant behaviour, it is actually a mask for lack of confidence in many cases.

So in order to increase both your competence and confidence, and then, in turn, to increase your resilience level, you should:

- pay attention to training and development for yourself;
- be clear about what your training needs are; and
- take steps to get the training and development you need.

Getting balance in your life – ensuring you have stability zones

The final element we need to look at to ensure a good level of resilience is balance. The notion of balance underpins most of what we have been saying about stress management. Getting a balance between the level of demand and the level of resilience is what will decide whether stress is experienced or not. Here we are talking about getting the balance right in your life between negative pressures and positive pleasures.

We have met many people who appear to give all their waking time to their work. We recognise that the world of work is changing and that working hours have increased for many people. During these past few years there has been growing concern about the fact that the UK has the longest working hours in Europe. There is now a Working Time Directive to ensure that reasonable hours are kept. This effectively restricts the working time of carers to a maximum of 48 hours a week. It is viewed as an unreasonable demand to expect employees to work too many hours.

The amount of time devoted to work is one aspect of 'balance', but an equally important issue is the use that is made of time outside work. We want to refer to the notion of 'stability zones'.

'Stability zone' is a phrase first coined many years ago by Alvin Toffler in a book called *Future Shock*. He originally used the phrase to illustrate how some people can cope well with the demands of change. Toffler's premise was that if at least some areas of our lives are stable, then we will be able to cope better with change. Hence our use of the word stability. It recognises the basic need for structure and stability in our lives. If there are some constants in our lives, we will deal better with change.

Stability zones are not only constants, they are where you get good feelings, recognition, and the joy of just being yourself. Don't forget that some of these pleasurable experiences can come from work, as well as play. Having good stability zones in your life will counter the negative experience of some of the demands you face in your role as carer.

Both demands and stability zones can take any form in our lives. It is too easy and far too simplistic to view the role of carer as where you get all the negative pressure, and outside work as where you get all the fun. This book is based on the premise that caring work is both rewarding and demanding. There will be positive aspects to your role as a carer. We invite you to take a moment to bring to mind what it is that you enjoy and find rewarding in the caring role. It is helpful to keep these rewards in mind, and remind yourself of them when things are tough.

Equally, it is tempting but unrealistic to view the whole of life outside the caring role as a stability zone. As we saw with Margaret, she was facing quite heavy demands from being a single parent with two growing children. It did not appear that her household was a great source of stability zones for her.

Stability zones can come in a wide variety of shapes and forms in our lives, linked to the role of carer, and to our lives outside that role. Stability zones can be tangible, such as a particular person or relationship; a particular place where you feel at home; or a particular object which is familiar and loved. Or stability zones can be less tangible, such as beliefs, perhaps religious or political, which give you a sense of purpose; or the feeling that something you do, like a hobby, or membership of an organisation, gives you an 'anchor'.

Thus stability zones can be linked to:

- People
- Places
- Things
- Ideas
- Activities
- Organisations

What stability zones do you have in your life?

It is important to have stability zones in your life, as without them it is easy to succumb to pressure. You need to be able to rely on them. Use this activity to think about what your stability zones are, and what you would like them to be.

ACTIVITY 13

This activity will take you about 20 to 25 minutes to complete. You'll need a quiet place to work, a pen or pencil, and a spare piece of paper. When you are ready, try to answer the following questions.

Identify your own stability zones

1 What values and beliefs do you hold which provide you with a secure base?

2 What places, large or small, provide you with roots or security?

3 Who are the people in your life on whom you can rely and who act as stability zones for you?

4 What are the things with which you feel comfortable and which act as stability zones?

5 What activities do you do which act as stability zones and anchors in your life?

6 What organisations or groups provide you with a sense of belonging?

Now look back over your answers, and see whether you can answer questions A, B, and C below.

A Do you need to change the pattern of your stability zones?

B Are there any changes you would like to make in the pattern of your stability zones? Do you have enough of them, are they reliable, and will they serve you in the future?

C If you have identified any changes you would like to make, how are you going to implement those changes?

Now that you have looked at the stability zones in your life, and identified ways in which you could strengthen your resilience by making some changes in how you use your time, we can move on to look in more detail at how you can plan ahead to manage your stress even more effectively.

In this chapter we have looked at:

- the need for support;
- the importance of training and development; and
- how balance can play a part in increasing resilience.

The key words we have identified as vital for resilience are support, competence, confidence and balance. Keeping these words in mind, and ensuring that you work towards getting the qualities they represent into your life, will stand you in good stead when facing pressure. In the next chapter we will look at ways of controlling your own personal response to stress.

KEY POINTS

- A good level of resilience helps us to withstand pressure.
- It is helpful to have positive attitudes towards looking after yourself.
- Getting support is a key aspect of resilience.
- It is a useful skill to be able to ask for support.
- Training and development increases competence and thus resilience.
- Focusing on developing your skills needs to be a lifelong process.
- Developing your skills increases confidence.
- Confidence helps you to deal with pressures.
- It is useful to have a good proportion of positive aspects ('stability zones') in your life, whatever kind of care work you do.
- The balance between positive and demanding aspects in your life is important.

7 Quick responses to dealing with stress

We have examined ways in which you can reduce unnecessary pressure and increase your resilience. By focusing on these two strategies, you will become better able to maintain a balance which is close to your optimum pressure level. Yet however well you plan and keep to a long-term strategy for managing your pressure level, there will always be moments when stress gets to you. Whether it's in the middle of dealing with a difficult service user, or in a meeting with your supervisor when you're just not getting your point across, or stuck in yet another traffic jam, there are countless occasions when stress can strike. In this chapter we will look at simple and effective techniques for reducing your blood pressure, quelling the urge to fight, and controlling your own personal response to stress.

We will start by examining ways in which you can use your creative abilities to deal with stress as it happens – by creating images which defuse the situation. We will then look at ways in which you can calm your body by various methods which contribute to relaxation. Finally we will look at ways in which you can defuse the pressure by releasing the tension you feel, safely, and under your own control.

Dealing with stress as it happens

There are a variety of techniques you can use to defuse stress as it happens. Some of them are suitable for use on the spot, as soon as you recognise that your stress response has swung into action. These are techniques that are not immediately apparent to anyone else but you. You can use them when with a service user, or with your manager, or with your friends and family. No-one around you will know what you are doing, but your system will know, and feel the difference. With other techniques you will need to wait a while until you are on your own, and can find a quiet moment in which to 'de-stress' yourself. These are techniques which need a little more concentration, time, and a place where you can be undisturbed for a while. It is useful to have both types of technique in your repertoire.

Pictures in the mind

The stress response starts in the mind. As we have explored, the very first step that triggers the stress response is the way a situation is viewed or experienced. A useful place to start to look for techniques to bring the stress response to a halt is thus the very place where it originated; in the mind. We may not have been aware that we were seeing someone as a large, dangerous beast, like the image of the mammoth we referred to in Chapter 1, but when the hands clench, and the voice rises and we feel the stirrings of fury at someone's obstinacy for example, it is as if a dangerous beast is being created by our mind.

So if the mind can trigger the stress response by how we perceive a situation, then it can also calm that response. All that is needed is a change of image. There are two ways in which this can be done. One involves humour; the other involves retreating in your mind to a favourite place.

Making the stressful silly

A very simple and easy technique is to add a dose of humour to the situation. There are a number of ways in which this can be done, but two have been well described and are widely used. They work best when the large dangerous beast currently facing you is in the form of an actual person.

As the hackles rise, look at the person who is getting to you, pause, blink and as you blink imagine them as an animal. As you pause, even just for the split second to do the necessary mental shift, you will be putting a pause into the build-up of pressure, and allowing a different perception to creep in. In a popular television programme of many years ago, whenever a certain character appeared, she was accompanied by the image of a hippopotamus. This showed how that character was seen by some members of her family. A hippopotamus is a slightly comical creature and it drew laughs from the studio audience. A hippopotamus can be dangerous in the wild, but creating the image of one in your mind can defuse a difficult encounter. Some people choose cats, using the image of a docile domesticated tabby to take the edge off the tension. To equip yourself to use this method, just pause and bring to mind some animal images which either bring a smile to your face, or make you want to go 'aaah'. Those are the images to use. Identify one which you like, and keep this in mind for the next difficult moment with another person.

The second way to introduce humour is to imagine the person who is causing you difficulty in a very ordinary or basic pose. Some people use the image of their adversary fast asleep and snoring. This image reduces the person to a very human and ordinary level and will defuse the tension for you.

Retreating to a nice place

The second technique that uses pictures in your mind involves creating images of a particularly nice, calming place for you. Take a moment to think about some of your favourite places. You could be thinking about a beach, a countryside scene, a mountainside, or any favourite haunt of yours, wherever and whatever it happens to be. Take a moment now to bring to mind a variety of images of places you know and love. Pay attention to your own response as you scan those favourite places in your mind's eye: the ones that bring on the contented sigh, or the smile of remembrance. When you have identified a couple which work for you, put them into your mental store-cupboard to keep for future use.

Images of favourite places work in the same way as the introduction of humour. As you catch yourself feeling the stress, pause, blink, and allow the image of your favourite place to enter your mind. This will take your attention away from what is actually happening, remind you of a pleasant place, and help to restore a sense of proportion into your reaction.

Calming the body down

Once the mind has perceived the 'mammoth', the body picks up the message and runs its normal course of gearing up for fight or flight. Thus the body will go into overdrive in terms of arousal level. There are a number of techniques for calming the body when the 'fight or flight' reaction is triggered.

The body is in a state of arousal caused by the 'sympathetic' nervous system. To put it simply, there are two sides to what is called technically our 'autonomic' nervous system – the 'sympathetic', which increases arousal, and the 'parasympathetic', which calms the body. The aim is to decrease arousal by consciously activating the 'parasympathetic' side of the nervous system. As the brain has already sent the signals warning of threat and danger, the body is already energised and alert. What is needed are techniques for calming down.

There are two ways by which the calming mechanism can be activated – relaxation and exercise. Both act as a 'switch' for the calming mechanism to come into effect.

Relaxing the body

There are many changes which happen as the body gears up to get out of danger. Many of them are not accessible to our conscious control, but two aspects of the physical changes brought about by stress are easy to bring under control. These are breathing and muscle tension.

Breathing is something we tend to take totally for granted. It happens automatically without us usually having to think about it. When stress strikes, however, we need to give it conscious thought. Whenever we are in the midst of a difficult situation, our breathing rate increases and becomes more shallow. This is to allow more oxygen to be brought into the lungs to deal with the immediate 'crisis'. You may not even be aware that your breathing rate has increased.

You can reverse the rapid, shallow breathing by slowing your breathing down. Pause and take a good deep breath. That will push air down to the bottom of your lungs and give your body the message that perhaps the situation is not so bad after all. Then breathe out strongly. It is the outbreath which calms. That is why we sigh with relief, as we release the air we have been holding. If we are startled, we breathe in sharply; when pleased we breathe out. So exhale forcefully. A few good slow deep breaths with strong exhalations will start the calming mechanism. This can be done without anyone else being aware of what you are doing.

Another technique which can be used without anyone else being aware of what you are doing, is to bring the **tension level in your muscles** under conscious control. As the stress response gets going, the tension in the muscles increases. This ensures that the vigorous physical actions of either running or fighting can happen. To reverse the process, relax the muscles. This is easier said than done.

First become aware of the build-up of tension in your muscles. You may feel it in your neck or find yourself clenching your fists or gritting your teeth. Wherever you feel the tension building, exaggerate the tension, and then let it go. Letting it go needs to be quite a strong movement. This is based on the principle that tension and relaxation are opposite states for the muscles. Tension is building anyway, so go with it to start with, and then consciously let it go. The body will react to the letting go of tension and again will get the message that perhaps the situation is not so bad after all. If you can relax your muscles, then the danger cannot be so great.

Calming the breathing and letting go of the tension in the muscles are the two main components of relaxation techniques. Once away from the immediate situation that brought on the pressure, you can take ten minutes or so to thoroughly relax yourself.

In order to **relax thoroughly**, either at the end of a long and hard day, or to prepare yourself for a good night's sleep:

- Find yourself a quiet spot where you will not be disturbed.
- Take up a comfortable position. (Many people say that they find this easier when in a semi-reclining position. Until you get more

familiar with the knack of thoroughly relaxing yourself, lying down or reclining is certainly the most helpful position.)

- Loosen any tight clothing and sink back into whatever you are sitting or lying on.
- Close your eyes and place a hand on your stomach, just below the ribcage.
- Breathe in deeply and allow the hand on your stomach to rise as the air is taken right down to the bottom of your lungs.
- Exhale slowly, and feel the hand fall.
- Do this a couple of times to get into the rhythm of breathing deeply and slowly.
- Then place your hand in a comfortable position and turn your attention to the different groups of muscles.
- Start with your feet. Concentrate on your feet and tighten the muscles in your feet. Hold for a few seconds and let the tension out.
- Repeat with tightening the muscles in your feet and letting go.
- Pause to recapture the deep, regular breathing pattern, then turn your attention to the muscles in your lower legs. Increase the tension, hold and then let go.
- Again, repeat it, and go back to your breathing.
- Gradually work up your body, through the upper legs, stomach, hands, arms, shoulders and face.
- Between tightening and relaxing each group of muscles, go back and focus on your breathing. The combination of deep, regular breathing and consciously easing the tension out of your muscles will lead to a feeling of being thoroughly unwound and relaxed.
- The final stage is to fill your mind with the image of a comforting, familiar object, person or place.

These three elements – breathing, relaxing the muscles and focusing your mind on a pleasant image – will lead to a warm, relaxed state. Thoroughly relaxing yourself is an excellent technique to use if you ever have difficulty sleeping, or whenever you need to slough off the pressures of the day. The more you practice and use it, the easier it will become.

Working the tension off – exercise

Relaxation techniques work by triggering our calming mechanism. So does exercise, which is the natural and ancient way of moving between the two parts of the autonomic nervous system – the energising (sympathetic) and the calming (parasympathetic). After all, when the fight or flight response was an appropriate way of responding to dangerous beasts, it was the physical action of running or fighting which calmed the body down. Nowadays we often hit problems because the traditional release is not available – or is it? We are not suggesting that you leap to your feet in the middle of a difficult situation and run out into the streets and do a marathon. But you can move. It is not helpful to stay absolutely stock still when the stress response is raging. Even if it is only walking briskly from one room to another, movement will help to calm the body down. So whenever you feel the signs of your personal stress response, start to move in whatever way is available to you at that moment.

If movement works to trigger the calming mechanism, then a longer bout of exercise can be an even more effective way of releasing stress and calming the body down. At the end of a long day, some form of exercise is most beneficial. It acts like fighting or running did for our ancestors, and restores the calming mechanism. By exercising the body systematically and safely, you will trigger the calming side. It need not take long – 15 or 20 minutes is enough to calm the body down.

There are various forms of exercise and it is essential that you choose one that suits you. There is no point in adding to the pressures you already face by inflicting another one on yourself, so find something you enjoy. There has been growing awareness in recent years of the benefits of regular exercise, and there are many forms readily available. Some people like to swim, others to cycle or walk. It has been said that the best form of exercise machine is a dog. While you are giving the dog its much-needed exercise, you too are getting yours. All of these forms of exercise are good ways to work the tension out of the body. They are not too strenuous and allow a regular, rhythmic pace to be built up. So to work the tension out of the body, movement at the time will help. Then you can progress to some form of exercise.

Exercise has much in common with the last group of techniques we shall look at. These are ways in which you can release the tension which stress creates. Exercise does that in a very direct and physical way. We go on now to look at less physical ways of releasing the tension.

Releasing the pressure

These techniques work to release pressure. They operate in a similar way to a pressure cooker, which has a valve to release pressure when it reaches a certain level. Exercise does this, but there are also other ways of releasing the pressure. Knowing how to release pressure can stop it building up over time.

Hitting a safe object

The basis of the stress response is frequently an urge to fight. We do not recommend that you pursue this urge. It helps, however, to understand that the wish to do battle is a common response to stress. It's one reason why slamming doors is such a frequent component of rows. One way of releasing the pressure is find a safe place and allow yourself to vent your wrath in safety. A very simple way of doing this is to hit a pillow or cushion. Place the pillow or cushion on a bed or chair. Make sure that you are not going to hit anything else by mistake as you hit the pillow. Then hit the pillow in short, sharp swings, letting the tension go down your arm and out of your fist.

There is a variation which can be added. This is to shout as you hit the pillow. It need not be a grammatical word, just a sound of releasing tension. It forces the air out of the lungs and strengthens the impact of releasing pressure. After you have spent some minutes releasing the pressure by hitting a pillow, we suggest you rest quietly.

Shouting inside your head

One colleague of ours visits the local golf driving range. As she hits each ball, she mentally places the person's name on it and says – 'this one is for you!' She finds it very therapeutic.

As this example shows, shouting and thereby releasing some tension can also be done inside your head. It may not be as effective as allowing the shout out, but it does have the advantage that you can use it when there are other people around who don't need to be know what is happening.

Shouting inside your head involves tuning in to the 'voice in your mind', rather than the mind's eye we were using earlier to create images. Turn up the volume silently to yourself; allow yourself to shout. Using a particular word can help. Some people find that shouting the word 'no' works for them. Others use the word 'stop'. This has the effect not only of releasing tension, but also of bringing yourself back into control of what is happening, and that in itself can help. So a silent shout can also release tension.

Writing it out

The final way of releasing tension we are going to look at is to let it out in writing. This is not a new technique, but one that remains a useful way of shifting the pressure from where it may be building up inside, and placing it outside yourself.

Whenever there is one particular thing that is getting you down, there may well be things that you would like to say, which are perhaps best left unsaid. This is where writing it down can help. However the idea of writing it down is *not* in order to give it to the person or people concerned; the aim is to move the pressure. That is what release is all about, moving the pressure from inside you to the outside world. But it needs to be done in a controlled and safe way.

Equip yourself with a piece of paper or a blank computer screen and write down everything you would like to say. Include everything you want to get off your chest. Keep it by all means, but it is not to be shared with whoever is the recipient in your mind (so take great care about how you store, or even destroy, what you have written, especially if the person 'in your mind' is in any sense close to you). This is *not* about sorting out a difficulty with another person; it is about releasing tension.

When dealing with an accumulation of many pressures, the simple activity of writing things down and transferring your inner feelings in a daily or weekly diary can be a way of releasing tension.

In this chapter, we have looked at ways in which you can quickly and easily deal with stress as it occurs. The three groups of techniques we have looked at – creating mental pictures, calming your body down and releasing the tension – will all work to keep you close to your optimum level of pressure. When you combine your knowledge of these 'first aid' techniques to manage stress with a long-term strategy for keeping your pressure balance under control, experiencing stress will hopefully become a rarer event in your life.

KEY POINTS

- It is useful to have quick and easy techniques to deal with stress as it happens.
- The first group of techniques involve creating pictures in the mind to defuse the tension.
- Creating a humorous image can stop the build-up of pressure.
- Retreating in your mind to a pleasant place can stop the effects of stress.
- The second group of techniques focus directly on calming the body down.
- Breathing deeply and regularly with forceful exhalations will relax the body.
- Letting go of muscle tension after first tightening the muscle will calm the body. Movement will also help.
- When away from the immediate situation, thorough relaxation and exercise will help counter the experience of stress.
- The final group of techniques focus on releasing the tension which is building up inside.
- Hitting a pillow or cushion in a safe place releases tension and can be accompanied by a shout.
- Shouting inside your head can also release tension.
- Writing all that you have ever wanted to say, but *not* passing it on to the other person, will also help to get the tension out of you.

8   Planning ahead

Now that we have looked at each of the components of the stress equation and explored the skills which are needed for effective stress management, in this chapter we will look ahead at how to plan for taking care of your pressure level in the future. Making changes, although not easy, can be simple and we suggest five steps to change which you can work through, perhaps with the help of a 'development buddy'.

Reading this book will have given you added insights into how you relate to pressure. Perhaps you have become more aware of how you respond to a pressure level that is wrong for you and perhaps you have gained by reflecting on the pressures you face. But above all we hope that reading this book has given you some new ideas of ways in which you can manage your pressure level.

You do not have to continue to suffer

One key point to emphasise is that whatever your experience of pressure and stress has been in the past, it is possible to develop new ways of dealing with it and managing yourself. If you have felt under pressure and have experienced more stress than you would like or than is good for you, you do not have to continue to suffer in the same way.

Above all else, having a sense of being more in control of your pressure should in itself increase your resilience. The trouble often starts when we feel weighed down and burdened by the demands of life at the same time as feeling unable to do anything about it. Being aware that there are strategies and techniques available to you, and that there are things you can do which do not involve a great deal of change but which can make a great deal of difference, will help you feel optimistic and hopeful about the future.

Therefore you do not need to go on in the same way as before.

Change is simple ...

Making changes in your life can often seem daunting. Change of any kind brings its own pressures. Change always involves pressures to adapt and to get used to a new way of doing things. However, the changes which we suggest are not major ones. You do not have to change your role, give up caring or move house in order to begin to plan for a life which provides optimum pressure without stress.

There may be elements of the care role you have which cause you problems, there may be times when you face difficulties, but there are ways of managing yourself through those. We do not recommend that anyone makes a big change, such as giving up your role as a carer, in the heat of the moment. What we do recommend is that you try out some of the techniques we have described and take some time in considering the smaller changes you can make, before making any major changes. Major change might be appropriate, but there is much that you can do before that becomes necessary.

We recognise that it is very easy for us to outline the different techniques which might be helpful for you. The key message is that they are easy to learn and practice. That is what we mean when we say that change is simple.

Five steps to change

Bringing about changes in your own patterns involves five steps, as illustrated on the next page.

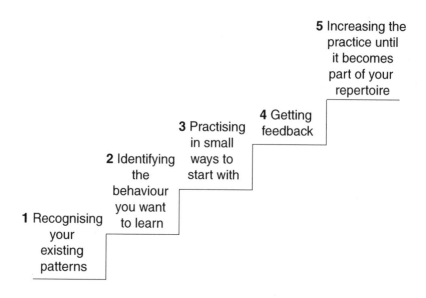

5 Increasing the practice until it becomes part of your repertoire

4 Getting feedback

3 Practising in small ways to start with

2 Identifying the behaviour you want to learn

1 Recognising your existing patterns

... but not easy

It sounds simple and in many ways it is simple. That does not mean that it will always be easy. Recognising your existing patterns of behaviour can be quite a searching activity. After all, they will be patterns which you have built up over years, perhaps without ever having taken a long hard look at what you do and how you do it.

Recognising the unhelpful messages we give ourselves can sometimes be quite painful. Gaining insight into how we do things often brings back memories of why we learnt to do things in that way in the first place. One person we worked with identified that she had a very strong internal message to 'be strong' and stand on her own two feet at all times. She found that as she grew to recognise this pattern in herself, it brought back memories of a parent who was not caring and who was not available for support. In this case she learnt to stand on her own two feet because she felt that there was no option. This was painful to recall, but also helpful in gaining understanding of how she had learnt to relate in this way in the first place.

So change is simple, but not always easy. That is why we suggest that you find a 'development buddy' to help you work through the five steps to change.

Working with a development buddy

When looking ahead and planning for the future it is always useful to get some support for yourself in this venture. This has been widely recognised in any programme of behaviour change, from slimming clubs to Alcoholics Anonymous. Getting support for behaviour change and having someone upon whom you can call combines in the notion of a 'development buddy' or a 'support buddy'.

When negotiating the arrangements with the person you choose, you need to be very clear about what you are asking for. We suggest that you negotiate to be in contact with them at regular intervals and have a clearly defined programme to talk about with them. It must, of course, be someone who is willing and prepared to take on this role with you. It is ideal if you are comfortable with your line manager fulfilling this function and they are willing and able to do it.

However if that is not possible, we have known many cases where two people have agreed to play this role for each other and the arrangement is reciprocal. In that case the sharing of the time needs to be divided equally. It can cause unnecessary bad feeling if one person feels that they are not getting the time and attention they need.

So think about the people you know and see who might be a suitable development buddy for you. If no-one comes to mind, just put it to the back of your mind and allow a name to emerge. You may find that you come up against some messages in the internal dialogue which get in the way, such as *'I have no right to ask'* or *'they wouldn't want to do it'*. This may be a good time to practice being clear about what you want, in your own mind at least. It is a good indicator that you are taking your stress management seriously, if you ask for support in dealing with it. Remember that you do not have to do everything on your own. We emphasised in Chapter 6 the importance of support in managing stress and we suggest that you ensure that you include this in your planning ahead. A development buddy is a good place to start.

Making a plan for the future

When thinking about how to manage your pressure level in the future, we suggest that you use the five steps to change, in conjunction with the three skills we have been exploring in this book of:

- recognising when stress is present;
- reducing unnecessary pressure; and
- increasing your resilience.

ACTIVITY 14

Planning for the future

The table on the next page plots these three skills against the five steps to change. Look at each of these skills, reflect on the thoughts which have crossed your mind while reading the book and then take each of the five steps in turn.

For example, when thinking about reducing unnecessary pressure, you may have recognised that your existing behaviour includes strong pressure on yourself to be perfect and to strive always for perfection. You may then choose to identify this as the behaviour which you would like to change. That would be a good time to meet with your development buddy to think about ways in which you could put this into practice. The practice steps need to be specific and measurable. Then decide on how you are going to get feedback. That includes giving yourself feedback. Then get together again and talk about how the practice went and how you will continue to practice the new behaviours. Monitoring progress with your development buddy is a good idea until you are confident that you really have achieved a new way of doing things.

That is just one example of how you can use this activity to help you to plan ahead. Follow this plan and you will be well equipped to stay stress free and work at an optimum level of pressure.

Five steps	Three skills: the ability to		
	Recognise stress	Reduce unnecessary pressure	Increase resilience
Recognise existing patterns			
Identify behaviours you want to change			
Plan to practice new behaviours			
Get feedback on the new behaviours			
Increase the practice			

We wish you well. Remember:

- you can ask for help;
- you do not have to do it all in a hurry;
- it does not have to be a great effort;
- you do not have to do what others want; and
- you do not have to get it all right.

We hope that you will continue to enjoy your care work and learn how to deal even more effectively with the demands.

KEY POINTS

- It is possible to change behaviour; you do not have to continue to suffer stress.
- Change in behaviour may not always be easy.
- Recognising existing patterns is a first step.
- You can then identify specific behaviour you want to change.
- Planning to practice a new way of doing things helps.
- Getting feedback on doing things differently is important.
- Increase your practice of the new ways until it is part of your repertoire.
- Find yourself someone to support you through the change process (a 'development buddy').
- Work out a specific step-by-step plan, focusing on the three skills of stress management.

Useful addresses

Action on Elder Abuse
1268 London Road
London SW16 4ER
Tel: 020 8764 7648
Elder Abuse Response: Freephone 0808 808 8141
Aims to prevent elder abuse. Operates a confidential helpline.

Alzheimer's Society
2nd Floor, Gordon House
10 Greencoat Place
London SW1P 1PH
Tel: 020 7306 0606
Information, support and advice about caring for someone with Alzheimer's disease.

Aromatherapy Organisation Council
PO Box 19834
London SE25 6WF
Tel: 020 8251 7912
For a list of qualified practitioners in your area.

British Acupuncture Council
63 Jeddo Road
London W12 9HQ
Tel: 020 8735 0400
For a list of acupuncturists in your area.

Association of Reflexologists
27 Old Gloucester Street
London WC1N 3XX
Tel: 0870 5673320
For names of reflexologists.

British Association for Counselling
1 Regent Place
Rugby
Warwickshire CV21 2PJ
Tel: 01788 550899
Publishes a directory of counsellors in the UK.

British Homeopathic Association
15 Clerkenwell Close
London EC1R 0AA
Tel: 020 7566 7800
For the names of homeopathic practitioners.

Carers National Association
20-25 Glasshouse Yard
London EC1A 4JT
Tel: 020 7490 8818
CarersLine: 0808 808 7777 (Mon to Fri, 10am–noon and 2–4pm)
Acts as the national voice of family carers, raising awareness and providing support, information and advice.

Centre for Study of Complementary Medicine
51 Bedford Place
Southampton SO1 2DG
Tel: 02380 334752
For advice and details of specialist organisations.

Coronary Prevention Group
2 Taviton Street
London WC1H 0BT
Tel: 020 7927 2125
Provides a range of information leaflets, newsletter and reading list.

Counsel and Care
Lower Ground Floor
Twyman House
16 Bonny Street
London NW1 9PG
Tel: 020 7485 1550
Advice line: 0845 300 7585 (10.30am – 4pm)
Offers free counselling, information and advice for older people and carers.

Drinkline
Tel: 0800 917 8282
National alcohol helpline that provides confidential information, help and advice about drinking to anyone, including people worried about someone else's drinking.

Health Development Agency
Trevelyan House
30 Great Peter Street
London SW1P 2HW
Tel: 020 7222 5300
Provides details of a wide range of leaflets and books promoting good health.

Quitline
Tel: 0800 002 200
A freephone helpline that provides confidential and practical advice for people wanting to give up smoking.

Sport England
16 Upper Woburn Place
London WC1H 0QP
Tel: 020 7273 1500
Publications: 0870 5210 255
Provides general information about all sports.

Stress Management Training Institute
Foxhills
30 Victoria Avenue
Shanklin
Isle of Wight PO37 6LS
Tel: 01983 868 166
Publishes a wide range of materials to help reduce stress: leaflets, audio tapes, books and a newsletter.

UK College for Complementary Health Care Studies
St Charles Hospital
Exmoor Street
London W10 6DZ
Tel: 020 8964 1205
For a list of qualified practitioners of therapeutic massage.

Further reading

Chaitow, L (1992). *The Stress Protection Plan*. Thorsons: London.

Cooper, CL, Cooper, RD and Eaker, LH (1988). *Living with Stress*. Penguin: London.

Goliszek, A (1993). *Sixty Second Stress Management*. Bantam Books: London.

Newell, S (1995). *The Healthy Organization*. Routledge: London.

Rice, P (1999). *Stress and Health*. Third edition. Brooks/Cole Publishing Company: California.

Saunders, C (1990). *Women and Stress*. Angus and Robertson: Australia.

About Age Concern

Staying Sane: Managing the stress of caring is one of a wide range of publications produced by Age Concern England, the National Council on Ageing. Age Concern works on behalf of all older people and believes later life should be fulfilling and enjoyable. For too many this is impossible. As the leading charitable movement in the UK concerned with ageing and older people, Age Concern finds effective ways to change that situation.

Where possible, we enable older people to solve problems themselves, providing as much or as little support as they need. A network of local Age Concerns, supported by 250,000 volunteers, provides community-based services such as lunch clubs, day centres and home visiting.

Nationally, we take a lead role in campaigning, parliamentary work, policy analysis, research, specialist information and advice provision, and publishing. Innovative programmes promote healthier lifestyles and provide older people with opportunities to give the experience of a lifetime back to their communities.

Age Concern is dependent on donations, covenants and legacies.

Age Concern England
1268 London Road
London SW16 4ER
Tel: 020 8765 7200
Fax: 020 8765 7211

Age Concern Cymru
4th Floor
1 Cathedral Road
Cardiff CF1 9SD
Tel: 029 2037 1566
Fax: 029 2039 9562

Age Concern Scotland
113 Rose Street
Edinburgh EH2 3DT
Tel: 0131 220 3345
Fax: 0131 220 2779

Age Concern Northern Ireland
3 Lower Crescent
Belfast BT7 1NR
Tel: 028 9024 5729
Fax: 028 9023 5497

Publications from Age Concern Books

Care professionals

CareFully: A handbook for home care assistants
Lesley Bell

Comprehensive and informative, this new edition of a highly acclaimed guide provides key advice for home care workers in promoting independence. Containing four totally new chapters, it is packed with practical guidance, detailed information on good practice and recent developments in home care provision. This new edition provides the underpinning knowledge for home carers for the S/NVQ level 2 revised units in care. Topics covered in full include:

- the importance of core values
- basic skills of home care assistants
- the health of older people
- receiving home care – the user's perspective
- taking care of yourself
- providing a service for the new millennium

Covering all of the key issues around the White Paper *Modernising Social Services* and complete with case studies and checklists, this is a book to enable all home care workers to face their job with confidence and enthusiasm.

£12.99   0-86242-285-X

Working with Family Carers: A guide to good practice
Jacqui Wood and Phill Watson

This multidisciplinary handbook is designed to enable care professionals to view family carers as perhaps their greatest resource and to work in partnership with them. It provides clear and detailed information on every aspect of working with carers, both practically and emotionally. The authors – both experienced practitioners – offer practical tips and experience, on topics such as:

- carrying out an assessment
- working with other agencies
- financial difficulties
- emotional and physical stress
- relevant legislation
- ensuring carers rights

Positive and supportive, this handbook will ensure that all front-line staff are fully armed in their fight to ensure carers receive the best possible support and help.

£14.99   0-86242-230-2

Health and care

Know Your Medicines
Pat Blair

This handy guide answers many of the common questions that older people – and those who care for them – often have about the medicines they use and how they work. The text stresses safety throughout, and covers:

- what medicines actually do
- using medicines more effectively
- getting advice and asking questions
- common ailments
- taking your medicine
- medicines and your body systems

There is also information about the dosage and strength, brands, storage and disposal and an index to help look up medicines that are prescribed or bought over the counter.

£7.99   0-86242-226-4

Caring for Ethnic Minority Elders: A guide
Yasmin Alibhai-Brown

A guide addressing the delivery of care to older people from ethnic minority groups, this book highlights the impact of varying cultural traditions and stresses their significance in the design of individual care packages. It looks at the broader framework of how elders receive care and then considers the requirements and experiences of ten distinct ethnic minority groups.

£14.99   0-86242-188-8

Money matters

Managing Other People's Money (2nd Edition)
Penny Letts

Foreword by the Master of the Court of Protection

Ideal for both the family carer and for legal and other advice workers, this new edition is essential reading for anyone facing this challenging situation. Providing a step-by-step guide to the arrangements which have to be made, topics include:

- when to take over
- the powers available
- enduring power of attorney
- Court of Protection
- claiming benefits
- residential care
- collecting pensions and benefits
- living arrangements

£9.99   0-86242-250-7

Your Rights: A guide to money benefits for older people
Sally West

Over the last 27 years, *Your Rights* has established itself as the clearest money benefits guide for older people. Updated annually, and written in jargon-free language, it has already helped more than 2.6 million people discover the full range of benefits available to them. Areas covered include:

- retirement pensions
- Housing and Council Tax Benefits
- benefits for disabled people
- funeral payments
- Income Support and the Social Fund
- paying for residential care
- paying for fuel, insulation and repairs
- help with legal and health costs

A highly successful, popular book, *Your Rights* ensures that older people – and their advisers – can easily understand the complexities of State benefits.

For more information please contact Age Concern Books in Devon.

If you would like to order any of these titles, please write to the address below, enclosing a cheque or money order for the appropriate amount (plus £1.95 p&p) made payable to Age Concern England. Credit card orders may be made on 0870 44 22 044 (individuals); 0870 44 22 120 (AC federation, other organisations and institutions).

Age Concern Books
PO Box 232
Newton Abbott
Devon TQ12 4XQR

Factsheets subscription/Information Line

Age Concern produces 44 comprehensive factsheets designed to answer many of the questions older people (or those advising them) may have. These include factsheets on money and benefits, health, community care, leisure and education, and housing. For up to five free factsheets, telephone 0800 00 99 66 (7am–7pm, seven days a week, every day of the year). Alternatively you may prefer to write to Age Concern, FREEPOST (SWB 30375), ASHBURTON, Devon TQ13 7ZZ.

For professionals working with older people, the factsheets are available on an annual subscription service, which includes updates throughout the year. For further details and costs of the subscription, please contact Pat Boon on 020 8765 2706, or write to her at Age Concern England's Head Office at the address on page 94.

Index